GEOGRAPHICALLY DISPERSED TEAMS

AN ANNOTATED BIBLIOGRAPHY

GEOGRAPHICALLY DISPERSED TEAMS

AN ANNOTATED BIBLIOGRAPHY

Valerie I. Sessa
Michael C. Hansen
Sonya Prestridge
Michael E. Kossler

Center for Creative Leadership
Greensboro, North Carolina

The Center for Creative Leadership is an international, nonprofit educational institution founded in 1970 to advance the understanding, practice, and development of leadership for the benefit of society worldwide. As a part of this mission, it publishes books and reports that aim to contribute to a general process of inquiry and understanding in which ideas related to leadership are raised, exchanged, and evaluated. The ideas presented in its publications are those of the author or authors.

The Center thanks you for supporting its work through the purchase of this volume. If you have comments, suggestions, or questions about any Center publication, please contact John R. Alexander, President, at the address given below.

Center for Creative Leadership
Post Office Box 26300
Greensboro, North Carolina 27438-6300

Center for
Creative Leadership
leadership. learning. life.

CCL No. 346

Library of Congress Cataloging-in-Publication Data

Geographically dispered teams : an annotated bibliography / Valerie I. Sessa ... [et al.].
    p. cm.
    Includes bibliographical references.
    ISBN 1-882197-54-2
    1. Teams in the workplace—Bibliography. 2. Communication in organizations—Bibliography. I. Sessa, Valerie I.

Z7164.O7 G38 1999
[HD66]
016.6584'02—dc21

                           99-047826

Table of Contents

Preface

Geographically dispersed teams (GDTs) create unique challenges to effective task performance and the development of interpersonal relationships among the members who serve on them. Separated by time and distance, GDT members must grapple with such issues as how people interact with technology, how distance (geographical, cultural, and temporal) affects teamwork, and how to communicate effectively when dispersed so widely.

Because the Center for Creative Leadership (CCL) wants to understand these challenges and help organizations and GDTs deal with them, it began a research project in 1997 to examine how organizations form, develop, and maintain GDTs.

To aid in developing research and training initiatives, the authors of this CCL report began to identify and compile the existing literature on GDTs. We consulted scientific and professional journals, articles published in the popular press, books, and Internet sources. The information we collected was so helpful to the purpose of developing CCL's research into GDTs, we decided it could also benefit others. Thus, we are providing our initial gathering of knowledge and understanding about GDTs in this annotated bibliography.

Our understanding of GDTs would not be possible without the foundation provided by the eighty-seven annotations in this literature review. We are grateful not just to the writers and thinkers and researchers whose labor and expertise helped lay that foundation, but also to CCL for publishing this report and disseminating this knowledge.

We specifically wish to thank the CCL staff members who helped make the project a reality. Marcia Horowitz suggested we write this report, read early drafts, and prodded us when we were slow. Peggy Cartner and Kinsey Gimbel of CCL's Library and Information Services group helped us identify and obtain many of the sources cited in this bibliography. Laurie Merritt devoted many hours of invaluable administrative support. Pete Scisco and Joanne Ferguson provided editorial and production expertise.

We are also grateful to David Loring, group director for Teams and Organizations at CCL; Jennifer Deal, research associate at CCL; and Vee Sutherland, of IBM Internal Transformation Consulting Services, for reading drafts of this report and providing insightful commentary and review.

Introduction

In the last decade, the way the world conducts business has changed dramatically. Regional markets have given way to global markets. Information and services have become currency and goods in their own right. No longer do businesses wait days and weeks for progress reports to arrive from remote work locations; instead, progress reports can be delivered in seconds and updated in real time. Communication and computer technologies are the great enablers, allowing workers, team leaders, and executives to literally see and hear associates on the other side of the globe and even in outer space.

Beyond enabling individuals, new technologies also enable organizations to better manage and utilize resources, both material and human. An example of this is the rapid increase in the use of and reliance upon geographically dispersed teams (GDTs).

A GDT has members dispersed across distance and time, who are linked together by some form of electronic communication technology, and who are only able to physically interact as a team on a limited basis. Advanced technology allows for such teams to function productively in the contemporary organizational environment.

Numerous issues and questions occur when launching new forms of intra- and interorganizational communication structures such as those employed by GDTs. People are perplexed by the technical questions involved in instituting GDTs; they want to know how interpersonal relationships among team members are affected by the nature of the team and its tools, and how to measure effective task performance in a GDT setting.

The purpose of this report is to provide an introduction to what the recent literature on GDTs says about these issues and others: how GDTs are similar to or different from co-located teams (CLTs); GDT advantages and disadvantages; and how to form, develop, and lead GDTs.

To help readers make sense of the information, we divided this report into three sections. In the Key Themes section, we outline the main GDT topics and issues arising from the literature. In the Annotated Bibliography section, we present the annotations in alphabetical order. Following the annotations, the Forming, Developing, and Maintaining GDTs section, based on research and findings in the literature, presents guidelines for professionals who must deal with the implementation and development of GDTs. Author and title indexes at the end of the book provide easy access to source material.

This report is for individuals charged with creating or leading GDTs, for designers who provide the technology for these teams, for trainers who are expected to help these teams develop and operate, and for organizational consultants called in to assist. In addition, organizational researchers will find the review of the literature helpful in developing their own ideas around GDTs.

Key Themes

Some general themes emerged from this body of multidisciplinary literature. Recommendations, research, and practitioner writings are still too new to draw very strong conclusions, although some relevant research is now more than a decade old. What we present here are ideas, suggestions, trends, surprises, and firsthand realizations.

Geographically dispersed collaboration is not new.

From tribal villages to military organizations, human groups have used whatever means at their disposal to communicate over distance. Smoke signals, drums, carrier pigeons, foot messengers—all of these have been employed at one time or another, and some still are. Christian Europeans, for example, established missionary outposts throughout the world to advance their collective goals. Then and now, ambassadors and emissaries carry national wishes to foreign counterparts. To this day, the mail (and its cousins, express delivery services) and the telephone remain critical in coordinating activities among groups and individuals separated by time and distance.

The need for dispersed groups and individuals to communicate and the ready adoption of ever more efficient communication tools to address that need are almost as old as human civilization itself. But what is new is the plethora of information and communication technology developed in the past few decades that has allowed GDTs to proliferate (Raisinghani, Ramarapu, & Simkin, 1998; Scrivener, 1994; Short, Williams, & Christie, 1976; Townsend, DeMarie, & Hendrickson, 1998).

Current organizational environments drive the use of GDTs.

Several sources speak to the changing organizational environment (Melymuka, 1997; Odenwald, 1996; O'Hara-Devereaux & Johansen, 1994; Snow, Davison, Snell, & Hambrick, 1996; Townsend et al., 1998). In today's global marketplace, organizations looking for a competitive edge often find it in technology that makes it possible for them to utilize their employees in ways almost unimaginable twenty or thirty years ago. Technology allows people and teams to work together in many ways, including the traditional same time, same place (face-to-face); same time, different place; different time, same place; and different time, different place.

Additionally, as many organizations (especially in the United States and in Europe) move toward service and information industries, they are empowering employees to share knowledge and to make decisions based on that shared knowledge. Global markets are driving organizations to seek competitive advantages through globalizing their operating procedures, maintaining a 24-hour work cycle, and recruiting and maintaining key human capital no matter where it exists—all with minimal lag time.

This new environment continues to change the way work gets done. It influences how a company chooses workers for a specific task. It affects how often those people collaborate and how interdependent their work is. Information and communication technology (e-mail, groupware, audio- and videoconferencing, shared editors, and databases) allow workers to rapidly exchange ideas and information, leading to a high frequency of collaboration and a greater interdependence among team members as they perform their tasks.

Knowledge about CLTs can be translated to GDTs.

GDTs are clearly an evolved form of team, not a new entity. The attributes that characterize co-located teams (CLTs) can, generally speaking, be applied to GDTs. In doing so, the dimensions by which GDTs and CLTs are similar and different can be understood more clearly. The literature on GDTs describes issues that can be categorized by input variables such as organizational inputs, group inputs, task characteristics, and individual team member inputs, along with processes associated with tasks and relationships and the outcomes that the team is expected to achieve.

Like CLTs, GDTs must frequently deal with inputs and constraints from the larger organization, including those involving technological infrastructure (Barua, Ravindran, & Whinston, 1997; Duarte & Snyder, 1999), training and technical support (Duarte & Snyder, 1999; Dwyer, Fowlkes, Oser, Salas, & Lane, 1997; Haywood, 1998; Henry & Hartzler, 1997; Jessup & Valacich, 1993), and the presence or absence of a supportive organizational culture (Conger, 1992; DeSanctis & Poole, 1994; Melymuka, 1997). GDTs must also address group inputs, such as the structure of the group (Duarte & Snyder, 1999; Galegher, Kraut, & Egido, 1990; Geber, 1995), its size (Jessup & Valacich, 1993), its composition (McGrath & Berdahl, 1998), and its norms (Geber, 1995). CLTs and GDTs both need to consider task characteristics—how to design the job (George, 1998; Henry & Hartzler, 1997) and, more specifically, the complexity of the task (Conger, 1992; Jessup & Valacich, 1993). The last cluster of inputs that require attention is that of individual inputs of team members, including competencies (Duarte & Snyder, 1999; Geber, 1995; Melymuka, 1997), attitudes (Grenier & Metes, 1995), and motives (Wilson, George, Wellings, & Byham, 1994).

In addition to contextual inputs, task and interpersonal relationship processes are obviously present in both types of team; these include communication (Armstrong & Cole, 1996; Galegher et al., 1990; Geber, 1995; Haywood, 1998; Straus, 1997), participation (McGrath & Hollingshead, 1994; Straus, 1996), degree of task activity (McGrath & Berdahl, 1998; Straus, 1997), and team cohesion (Geber, 1995; Straus, 1997). Finally, CLTs and GDTs have expected outcomes in common, including the quality and quantity of output (Bordia, 1997; Jessup & Valacich, 1993; McGrath & Hollingshead, 1994; Nunamaker, Briggs, Mittleman, Vogel, & Balthazard, 1996), their long-term survival, and individual and collective developmental issues (Johansen, Sibbet, Senson, Martin, Mittman, & Saffa, 1991; McGrath & Hollingshead, 1994; Reinig, Briggs, Shepherd, Yen, & Nunamaker, 1995).

GDTs are different from CLTs in two major ways.

First, the medium on which each of these kinds of teams depends to accomplish its task differs. Traditional CLTs primarily meet in a same-time, same-place environment, using the medium of face-to-face meetings. By their very nature, GDTs rarely operate in this kind of environment. A second and related difference is that GDTs depend heavily on information and communication technologies (including but not limited to videoconferencing, audioconferencing, e-mail, telephone, fax, white boards, and the Internet) as the medium for facilitating meetings. Therefore, although GDTs and GDT leaders deal with issues similar to the ones faced in CLTs, how those issues are addressed may be quite different (Jessup & Valacich, 1993; Olson, Olson, & Meader, 1997; Oravec, 1996; Postmes, Spears, & Lea, 1998).

Traditional team processes are more difficult for GDTs.

Communication and coordination is different and often more difficult in a GDT than in a CLT (Barua et al., 1997; Bordia, 1997; Galegher et al., 1990; Hightower & Sayeed, 1994; McGrath & Hollingshead, 1994; McLeod, Baron, Marti, & Yoon, 1997). For example, working in a geographically dispersed fashion leads to GDT members behaving differently than they would if working in close proximity as a CLT. GDT members are less socially inhibited and less hierarchical than their CLT counterparts, which in turn influences other team factors: people are less likely to change their choices, for example, and discussion biases are more prevalent. Explicit coordination becomes more important. Some mixed evidence suggests that working in a dispersed fashion either inhibits the development of trust (Geber, 1995; Handy, 1995) or that trust develops differently (Coutu, 1998; Jarvenpaa,

Knoll, & Leidner, 1998) within a dispersed group than an undispersed one. These differences have an impact on both task and social processes, both of which in turn are affected by time and distance. As GDTs become more commonplace and workers grow accustomed to operating in a dispersed environment, team processes may become similar to those in CLTs.

The GDT's impact on task-related processes. GDT members communicate with each other less often than do CLT members, but their communications are often more task oriented (McGrath & Berdahl, 1998; Straus, 1997). GDTs have more equal participation among members than do CLTs, although some members participate more and have more influence than other members (Straus, 1996; Weisband, Schneider, & Connolly, 1995). GDTs take longer to accomplish their goals (Bordia, 1997; Graetz, Boyle, Kimble, Thompson, & Garloch, 1998; McGrath & Hollingshead, 1994) and have a harder time dealing with conflict and achieving consensus than do CLTs.

The GDT's impact on social-related processes. Because the effect of dispersion on socio-emotional processes within a team has not been explored as fully as the impact on task processes, there are few conclusive findings. Some literature suggests that dispersion enabled by various forms of technological media alters social behavior because it removes social boundaries (Bordia, 1997; Raisinghani et al., 1998). Other researchers and writers suggest that such dispersion and communication solidifies social boundaries (Postmes et al., 1998). It does seem that dispersion results in less social interaction among teams (McGrath & Berdahl, 1998); this lack of interaction may result in team members having inaccurate perceptions of other team members and of the task (Bordia, 1997; Reinig et al., 1995), and fostering weaker relational links (Warkentin, Sayeed, & Hightower, 1997). This reduced social activity may result from the inability of communication technologies to effectively and efficiently transmit social context cues (such as tone of voice, facial gestures, or body language), making it difficult for team members to bond (Hinds & Kiesler, 1995; Kling, 1996; Storck & Sproull, 1995). However, other research suggests that GDT members can pass along social context cues through communication technology (Lea & Spears, 1992). As time passes, GDT members may process socio-emotional information with greater effectiveness (Walther, 1994, 1995; Walther & Anderson, 1994).

The effect of distance and time on GDTs. Time seems to be key for both the task and the social processes of teams (Bordia, 1997; McGrath & Berdahl, 1998; Walther, 1994; Walther & Anderson, 1994). GDTs typically take more time to accomplish assignments, particularly when teams are new.

There is evidence, however, suggesting that as GDT members grow accustomed to working in a dispersed environment, the time it takes the team to produce solutions and accomplish tasks becomes equal to the time spent by CLTs. Additional evidence suggests that social processes also develop over time, especially when GDT members anticipate being in the group for an extended period of time (Igbaria & Tan, 1998). Much of the research evidence available looks at GDTs at only one point in time (that is, while performing a single task) rather than examining them over an extended period of time. The few studies available that do take time into account reinforce the notion that, after a while, task and social processes run more smoothly. For organizations working with intact GDTs, the effect of time is good news: GDTs can be effective and do not compromise performance. For researchers, sorting out the findings (which are inconclusive) related to the impact of time on GDTs remains a challenge.

The quality of output is the same for GDTs and CLTs.

Differences in processes do not appear to adversely impact the team's productivity. Generally, there is no difference in the quality of outcome between GDTs and CLTs, especially when the time factor is taken into account (Chidambaram & Jones, 1993; McGrath & Berdahl, 1998; Straus, 1996). GDTs may have difficulty dealing with negotiations or problem solving, but tend to do a better job of generating ideas than do CLTs (Aiken & Vanjani, 1997; Bordia, 1997; McGrath & Hollingshead, 1994).

GDT members experience less satisfaction than CLT members.

Research indicates GDT members are not as satisfied as CLT members (Galegher et al., 1990), although there are exceptions (Aiken & Vanjani, 1997). The reason for dissatisfaction may be the loss of the "human moment" which Hallowell (1999) describes as an authentic psychological encounter that is difficult to achieve without face-to-face meetings.

GDTs may take longer to develop.

There is some evidence that GDTs develop in stages—similar to the ways CLTs develop (Bordia, DiFonzo, & Chang, 1999; Igbaria & Tan, 1998; Johansen et al., 1991). However, they proceed through the stages of development more slowly, and differently, than existing theories of group development predict.

There are individual and organizational advantages to using GDTs.

Throughout the literature, many discussions emerge about the advantages of GDTs over CLTs, including: (1) Organizations achieve better use of human resources (access to experts and job candidates regardless of location, added depth of knowledge, and a round-the-clock workforce). (2) Individual employees gain opportunity for travel, greater job flexibility, and increased independence (presumably leading to a reduction in team and organizational hierarchy and higher levels of participation). (3) Organizations gain cost reductions, reduced office space, and less redundancy in resources. However, it needs to be acknowledged that GDTs are not the answers to all problems in organizations. GDTs should only be implemented when they are the best option for the problem to be solved. Although GDTs offer wonderful potential, they are not easy to form and develop, even in the most desirable situations.

GDT practice precedes science.

Researchers are learning about GDTs even as organizations are forming them out of competitive necessity. The field of GDT study begs for the collaborative efforts of social scientists (anthropologists, sociologists, and psychologists), design experts, and business experts to plan how to study the phenomenon, how to best design GDT-based interventions, and how to facilitate the work of these teams. That said, it must be noted that the current study of GDTs offers little utility for organizations struggling to implement and manage them. For example, teams are rarely completely co-located or completely dispersed. Usually, they exist somewhere between these two situations. Likewise, GDT members rarely meet in a purely dispersed fashion; they often meet face-to-face at the beginning of the project or over the course of the project. Sometimes a few members may work in the same location, but the team itself is still considered a GDT.

Alternatively, CLTs often rely on communication technology such as e-mail or voice mail as much as they count on face-to-face meetings. Such teams may employ conferencing technology if a key member is traveling or working from home. In collecting and annotating the literature about GDTs, we have found that much of the current research looks only at the ends of the continuum, at teams that meet face-to-face or at teams that are completely dispersed. Studies that we have cited here tend to examine individuals who come together for one meeting and who use technology with which they are unfamiliar. This view, as reflected in the literature, leads us to wonder how valid the findings may be for those who are actually experiencing GDT use in organizations.

Annotated Bibliography

Books and Journals

The annotations here reflect readings from a wide variety of sources identified through *PsychLit* and *ABI Inform* databases (using researcher name and such topics as *virtual teams*, *geographically dispersed teams*, *global teams*, *computer-supported collaborative work*, and others), recommendations from colleagues, and reference sections of the literature we read. The sources can be characterized as scientific journal articles, articles from the popular press, books, book chapters, essays and viewpoint essays from practitioners and experts in the field, and on-line publications located on the Internet's World Wide Web.

We had several rules for deciding whether or not to include a citation in these annotations. First, the material had to be directly related to GDTs (we did not, however, include reports that critiqued specific technical tools). Articles had to be current (published in the 1990s) or be considered classics (cited often in the subsequent literature). We specifically included sources that addressed issues related to forming, developing, and maintaining GDTs. Further, we judged each source as to whether it contributed important infor mation to the GDT topic. Although we looked for academic rigor in the articles published in scientific journals, we did not discriminate on this variable. Because the area is relatively new and sources were evident in a variety of literature, with varying rules for rigor, we decided to be as inclusive as possible.

We also decided not to include references to culture and its impact on GDTs. The reasons behind this choice were twofold: to include GDT issues related to culture would have made this project unmanageable, and some of our CCL colleagues are already exploring the impact of culture on leadership issues (Wilson, Hoppe, & Sayles, 1996 [see reference list]).

The content of each annotation varies by source. In general, we included the objective and a summary of contents. If the source reported on research, we included a description of the study's hypotheses, procedures, and findings.

The terminology surrounding the study of GDTs deserves special note. Throughout our reading, we found a lot of new language that has developed around using technology in teams, for which no standard vocabulary exists. Many different words cover a small set of new phenomena. Terms like *virtual*, *geographically dispersed*, *global*, and *transnational* are used interchangeably—sometimes within the same sentence—to describe teams that work across distance and time while communicating electronically.

In an attempt to provide a coherent set of vocabulary to simplify the readings in this annotated bibliography, we offer the following suggestions.

Team is an aggregation of two or more people working interdependently toward a goal and who are in a dynamic relationship with one another. Another word used similarly to *team* is *group*.

Geographically dispersed teams (GDTs) are teams whose members are dispersed across distance and time, are linked together by some form of electronic technology, and physically interact with each other rarely or not at all. Other terminology with similar connotations includes *virtual teams*, *computer-mediated teams* (when not co-located), *remote teams*, and *global transnational* or *international teams*. Globally distributed teams, as characterized in the latter two terms, add the distinction of work "spanning multiple countries."

Co-located teams (CLTs) are teams typically operating in the same location with close physical proximity, whose members can have face-to-face contact on a regular basis. Other terminology reflecting the same meaning includes *face-to-face teams*.

Aiken, M., & Vanjani, M. (1997). A comparison of synchronous and virtual legislative session teams faced with an idea generation task. *Information & Management, 33,* 25-31.

    The objective of this research was to compare idea generation between CLTs and GDTs. Eighty-nine undergraduate business students, divided into ten teams, took part in the study. All of the teams were asked to generate solutions to a parking problem on a university campus. The team members in the GDT group were split between two rooms. The team members in the CLT group remained together. Both kinds of teams were provided with idea-generation software to support their task work. The GDT groups generated a greater number of unique comments during idea generation than did the CLT groups. GDT members said they were more satisfied with the technology, and believed their comments were more anonymous than did the CLT members.

* * *

Armstrong, D. J., & Cole, P. (1996). Managing distances and differences in geographically distributed work teams. In S. E. Jackson & M. N. Ruderman (Eds.), *Diversity in work teams: Research paradigms for a changing workplace* (pp. 187-215). Washington, DC: American Psychological Association.

    These authors conducted a case study of an organization utilizing GDTs. The research involved reviews of group documents and interviews with thirty-eight managers, individual contributors, and staff consultants from nine GDTs. These were integrated with previous research to present a broad view of the factors that influence teams working in distributed environments. The authors discussed the role of electronic communication on team dynamics and the relationships and conflicts that exist among corporate, national, home office, and remote site cultures. The chapter discusses the influence of time and distance on (voluntary) group development. A key variable in this process, psychological closeness among members, is composed of: (1) the degree of identification with group membership; (2) the similarity of work goals, norms, role, and procedure expectations (task cohesion); (3) the accuracy of mutual comprehension; (4) the degree of motivation toward shared goals; (5) the amount of interdependency and mutual trust; and (6) the frequency of communication of members. Based on these variables, a group can find success through effectively structured leadership and management practices, group learning, and developing team norms related to cultural differences and the use of technology. It is interesting to note that the size of the teams in this study ranged from 25 members to 450, suggesting that in evaluating findings about GDTs it is important to take into consideration the size of the group being examined.

***

Barua, A., Ravindran, S., & Whinston, A. B. (1997). Coordination in information exchange between organizational decision units. *IEEE Transactions on Systems, Man, and Cybernetics: Part A. Systems and Humans, 27,* 690-698.

This article discussed the problem of coordinating information during communications between business units. The authors defined the problem as an information exchange in which attributes required by the receiver and attributes provided by the sender do not match. One example discussed occurred at Land's End, a mail-order company. In that example, one business unit provided garment sales information by style while another unit required that this information be categorized by color and size. This paper suggested that uniformity in information management capability and information technology resources are necessary across the organization to ensure efficient information coordination among GDTs.

***

Bordia, P. (1997). Face-to-face versus computer mediated communication: A synthesis of the experimental literature. *The Journal of Business Communication, 34,* 99-121.

The author reviewed eighteen published experimental studies that compared CLTs with GDTs on a variety of dimensions and described several findings: there is reduced normative social pressure in GDTs and a higher incidence of uninhibited behavior; perception or understanding of other group members and the task to be completed is poorer in GDTs; there is greater equality of participation in GDTs; GDTs perform better than CLTs on idea-generation tasks; GDTs exhibit less choice shift or attitude change; GDTs take longer to complete tasks; in a given time period, GDTs produce fewer remarks than CLTs; when time is limited, GDTs perform better on tasks involving less socio-emotional interaction and worse on tasks requiring more such interaction as compared to CLTs; when time is limited, evaluation of other group members is poorer in GDTs; and evaluation of the communication medium is influenced by the type of task. The author also provided an evaluation of the studies and suggested that because many of the studies used students who were unfamiliar with the computer-mediated technology and who were expected to interact over a short amount of time, findings may be due to design considerations.

***

Bordia, P., DiFonzo, N., & Chang, A. (1999). Rumor as group problem solving: Development patterns in informal computer-mediated teams. *Small Group Research, 30,* 8-28.

One of the objects of this study was to look at group development in GDTs using Wheelan's (1994; see reference list) developmental model with five stages: (1) dependency and inclusion, (2) counterdependency and flight, (3) trust and structure, (4) work, and (5) termination. Researchers used a larger study focusing on rumor transmission on the Internet. For this study they examined fourteen GDTs naturally arising on the Internet due to rumors (stories about computer viruses, for example). Findings suggest that GDTs develop similarly to CLTs in content but differ in the rate that they pass though the developmental cycle.

***

Chidambaram, L., & Jones, B. (1993). Impact of communication medium and computer support on group perceptions and performance: A comparison of face-to-face and dispersed meetings. *MIS Quarterly, 17,* 465-491.

The object of this research study was to determine the impact that electronic meeting systems (EMS) had on CLTs and GDTs (using audioconferencing) in terms of perceptions and actual team performance. Twenty-four teams of three or four students each participated in both a CLT meeting and a GDT meeting. In half of the CLT meetings, teams used an EMS. In half of the GDT meetings, teams used an EMS. Findings indicated that there was no difference in the quality of the decision process, the number of alternatives generated, or the quality of the final decision between CLT meetings and GDT meetings. The addition of an EMS to both CLT and GDT meetings had a positive impact on the quality of the decision process and the number of alternatives generated but did not have an impact on the quality of the final decision. Interestingly, the introduction of EMS was met with mixed perceptions within CLTs and GDTs—some positive and some negative. Teams meeting face-to-face, CLTs, felt less "social presence" (feeling the presence of other communicators) using EMS than when not using EMS, while EMS had no impact on social presence in GDTs. GDTs felt that communication was better when they used EMS; GDTs that did not use EMS reported poorer communication. There were no differences in communications effectiveness reported by teams that met face-to-face.

***

Conger, S. (1992). An exploration of the use of information technologies for inter-unit coordination. In R. S. Stollenmaier (Series Ed.) & U. E. Gattiker (Ed.), *Technological innovation and human resources: Vol. 3. Technology-mediated communication* (pp. 63-115). New York: Walter de Gruyter.

This chapter described a survey research project that asked employees from a variety of industries to provide information about the following: their use of information technology (face-to-face meetings, electronic messaging, telephone, databases, shared applications) to coordinate work with others outside their own units, how much the organizational cultures supported information technology, and the complexity of the tasks performed. Based on a hypothetical model, it was expected that as task complexity intensifies, employees would be more likely to use information technology that provides feedback (for example, audio- and videoconferencing, meetings, electronic messaging) and less likely to use information technology that does not provide feedback (databases and faxes, for example). This expectation was based on the idea that the feedback possible in audioconferencing and meetings, for example, allows for the coordination necessary for highly complex tasks, while such technology as shared databases and faxes lack the necessary feedback opportunities for coordinating complex tasks.

In addition, it was expected that the more complex the tasks within an organization, the less likely the organizational culture would support information technology. The author suggested that there is a bias in organizations toward using technology for simple, stable tasks, while using meetings and telephones for complex tasks. Finally, a positive information-technology culture was expected to be positively related to information technology use and negatively related to non-information technology use. Thus, task complexity was expected to have a direct effect on the type of coordination method and an indirect effect, through the organizational culture, on information technology use.

Using a sample of 105 employees from twenty-three banking, financial services, and insurance companies, these hypotheses were generally supported. While the relationship between task complexity and information technology has been frequently studied, the author recommended greater research attention be paid to the attitude of corporate culture toward information technology. Furthermore, recommendations for managers included: implement information technology to implicitly support its use; provide training and ongoing support; explain how information technology is expected to contribute to the future of the organization through strategy statements, operating plans, and job descriptions; adjust career planning to promote the learning of information technology skills; and make a variety of information technology accessible for complex tasks. Based on the context of inter-unit coordination, these findings may be especially appropriate for cross-functional teams.

***

Corbin, C. (1997, November). Tips to ensure good communication in a virtual office. *Workforce: Workforce tools supplement,* pp. 4-5.

The author offered several suggestions for enhancing communication in the virtual office, which are also important for GDTs: communicate regularly, establish communication times, make certain that all group members under-stand their worth, and have official and social events periodically so that members can meet face-to-face for business and social reasons.

***

Coutu, D. L. (1998, May-June). Trust in virtual teams. *Harvard Business Review,* pp. 20-21.

The authors reported that trust does not evolve slowly in GDTs. It tends to be established, or not, at the outset. The first interactions are crucial. Teams with the highest level of trust shared three traits. First, they began their interactions with an "electronic courtship," a series of social messages before focusing on the task. Second, they set clear roles for each team member. Third, the team members consistently displayed eagerness, enthusiasm, and an intense action orientation in their messages.

***

Dennis, A. R., Tyran, C. K., Douglas, R., & Nunamaker, J. F., Jr. (1997). Group support systems for strategic planning. *Journal of Management Information Systems, 14,* 155-184.

This article discussed the application of group support systems (GSS) to strategic planning tasks and described a study conducted to evaluate the effectiveness of the GSS capabilities for subtasks of the strategic planning process. The authors argued that group support systems have capabilities that involve process support, process structure, task support, and task structure. These capabilities are spread across a number of tools built into GSS: explo-ration and idea-generation tools, idea-organization tools, prioritizing tools, and policy-development and evaluation tools. The authors collected data ranging from case reports, final reports from facilitators, transcripts of elec-tronic communication, organization planning documents, and corporate annual reports from thirty organizations using GSS. The authors sought to answer research questions regarding the extent to which the four capabilities of GSS affect strategic planning success factors, including information production and identification, communication and integration of information, flexibility, and leadership. Process support appeared to be most strongly linked to planning success—factors, production and identification, communication, and integration—while task structure was the only significant influence on flexibility and leadership success factors.

***

DeSanctis, G., & Poole, M. S. (1994). Capturing the complexity in advanced technology use: Adaptive structuration theory. *Organization Science, 5*, 121-147.

Adaptive structuration theory (AST) attempts to create a dynamic model of how people incorporate and adopt technology into their social work environment. Rather than a purely rational model of technology use, which is represented in the decision-making school of thought, AST posits that social practices combine and interact with the structure of technology to determine the impact on behavior. This article outlined the groundwork for AST (an integrated model based on decision-making and institutional schools of thought), stated propositions for AST-guided research, and described the use of AST in the analysis of group-decision support system use. Based on the major constructs and propositions of AST, the authors created a model that hypothesized how the structural features and spirit of technology, other sources of structure, and a group's system of interaction influences how a group uses technology, makes decisions, and develops new structures. Investigating the subtle interplay of technology and social processes can clarify how multiple outcomes can result from implementation of the same technology and explain the inconsistent findings regarding the impact of advanced technologies.

***

Duarte, D. L., & Snyder, N. T. (1999). *Mastering virtual teams: Strategies, tools, and techniques that succeed.* San Francisco: Jossey-Bass, 229 pages.

This practitioner-oriented book is based on three sources of information: (1) the authors' own experiences and practice in working with GDTs, (2) academic and applied literature in the area of computer-supported cooperative work (CSCW), and (3) recent management and organizational behavior literature on teamwork and boundary management. From these sources, the authors put together a book that discusses what GDTs are (and how they compare and contrast to CLTs), how to create GDTs, and how to make GDTs successful. This book includes suggestions, checklists, and worksheets for the practicing leader of such teams. In the first section, the authors outlined different types of GDTs, including: networked, parallel, project or product-development, work or production, service, management, and action. They also listed seven critical success factors for GDTs: technology, human resources policies, training and development for leaders and members, standard organizational and team processes, organizational culture, leadership, and leader and member competencies.

The authors' description of the various types of teams and success factors provided the framework for the remainder of the book. In the second section, they discussed leader competencies needed (performance management and coaching, appropriate use of information technology, managing across cultures, career development and transition, building trust, networking, and developing and adapting standard team processes), member competencies (project management, networking, use of technology, self-management, boundary management, and interpersonal awareness), and the steps needed to start a GDT (identifying sponsors, stakeholders, and champions; developing a team charter; selecting and contacting team members; team development and orientation; and developing team processes). In the final section, the authors outlined GDT dynamics such as how to hold meetings and working adaptively.

***

Dwyer, D. J., Fowlkes, J. E., Oser, R. L., Salas, E., & Lane, N. E. (1997). Team performance measurement in distributed environments: The TARGETs methodology. In M. T. Brannick, E. Salas, & C. Prince, *Team performance assessment and measurement: Theory, methods, and applications* (pp. 137-153). Mahwah, NJ: Lawrence Erlbaum Associates, 384 pages.

In this chapter, the authors argued that because many teams work in distributed environments, team training should also take place in a distributed setting. They described the development and implementation of an event-based training and measurement technique called Target Acceptable Responses to Generated Events or Tasks (TARGETs) supported by Distributed Interactive Simulation (DIS) technology. DIS is a joint effort by government, industry, and academia to develop multiple simulation systems. This distributed training technique was tested with aviation teams in a complex simulated mission. Observers rated training performance on routine tasks and events with high reliability, but rated reliability for dynamic events and nonroutine tasks with modest reliability. The researchers acknowledged that the DIS technology needs to mature.

***

Fisher, K., & Fisher, M. D. (1998). *The distributed mind.* New York: AMACOM, 288 pages.

This book is about knowledge work and knowledge work teams. Its purpose was to address specific challenges that knowledge work teams face. Findings are drawn from interviews with knowledge workers. Many of the chapters are illustrated using case stories from individuals who serve on such teams. The authors defined knowledge work as any work that requires mental power rather than physical power. Such work has significant challenges, including self-management; developing information acquisition and transfer systems; employing multiple skills; and dealing with new team members, outsiders, and limited resources.

Although the authors covered many topics in this book, they specifically addressed GDTs in one chapter, providing suggestions for leading such teams. The authors believed that leaders need to manage the boundaries. To do so, leaders should articulate a vision; manage by principle rather than policy; coach, understand, and communicate information; eliminate barriers to effectiveness; facilitate and develop team members; and focus on the customer's perspective. Within the team, members lead by rotating leadership, sharing leadership, or distributing leadership. The authors concluded in this chapter that GDTs differ a great deal from CLTs because they are typically part-time, short-term teams with shifting membership from multiple locations (a notion not supported in other literature collected in this annotated bibliography).

***

Galegher, J., Kraut, R. E., & Egido, C. (Eds.). (1990). *Intellectual teamwork: Social and technological foundations of teamwork.* Hillsdale, NJ: Lawrence Erlbaum, 552 pages.

The goal of this edited volume was to "demonstrate the mutual relevance of social science and the design of information systems and to encourage better integration of those disciplines." The editors believed that developing a multidisciplinary body of work on teams and technology can provide guidance to those who design technological systems for teams and to those who attempt to use technology within teams. To achieve these aims, the editors divided the book into four sections. In the first section, they discussed the fundamental social properties of teams in organizations that need to be taken into account by those developing technology and by those using it. Topics included temporal aspects of teams, the structure of teams, working relationships, and mutual knowledge. The second section switched from specific topics to specific teams and included field studies of teams in organizations working on intellectual tasks. These teams included those working on research, new products, navigation, and medical diagnosis. Together, these two sections provided a basic understanding of collaborative work in teams, both from a theoretical point of view and from a descriptive point of view.

The book's third section included empirical investigations of teams that used technology. These studies described how technology impacts team structures, coordination, communication, and performance. Findings suggested that electronically supported teams develop a rich communication structure that is different from (and supplemental to) more traditional communication structures, with less hierarchical differentiation, broader participation, and more fluctuating and situational leadership structures. Time and space constraints are also less limiting in these kinds of teams. There was some indication that the performance of teams was enhanced by the use of technology, although in some cases group members were less comfortable and less confident in their conclusions. The book's final section looked forward to new technologies (those on the horizon in 1990).

* * *

Geber, B. (1995, April). Virtual teams. *Training, 32*(4), 36-40.

This article discussed how companies that use GDTs are finding that to ensure the success of team projects, they must pay attention to human factors. The author identified three "formidable interpersonal barriers" to GDT effectiveness: (1) lack of understanding and personal trust among members, (2) team member competence, and (3) information hoarding.

To overcome these barriers, the author suggested seven rules: (1) periodically get team members together face-to-face to improve the chances for serendipity; (2) provide GDTs with *more* formal communications, not fewer; (3) keep a record of past communication so that new members have access to the group's work history and don't threaten the group's cohesion; (4) use rigorous project-management principles, such as being as specific and direct as possible in determining missions, assignments, and deadlines; (5) establish norms and agreements about how the team will operate and how it will communicate electronically; (6) create a team leader (formally called a manager) and a team facilitator; and (7) choose team members carefully (look for people who are comfortable sharing information and working with computers; people with strong personalities who can assert themselves in an electronic medium; and people who can empathize with others).

***

George, J. A. (1998). Virtual best practice: How to successfully introduce virtual team-working. In G. M. Parker (Ed.), *Handbook of best practices for teams,* Vol. 2 (pp. 447-464). Amherst, MA: HRD Press.

To help organizations deal with planning and organizing the work of virtual teams and the variety of technical expertise, organizational functions, and time zones that often accompany them, the author suggested a number of best practices gleaned from a selection of organizational examples. When companies hurry to implement virtual teams, which are defined here by any of three components (geographical dispersion, different functions, and different duration of team existence), they may underestimate the need to plan and design around the differences inherent in virtual teams. Because of this lack of planning team members may collide, exhibiting coordination, group dynamic, and leadership problems based on a lack of trust, unrealistic or unequal expectations, and cultural differences.

Five best practices important for successful virtual teams fall under the themes of (1) organizational design, (2) job design, (3) interaction with stakeholders, (4) coordinating work through technology, and (5) reentry. Organizational design involves defining business goals, putting team values into action, and establishing team boundaries. Job design principles include building an entire product process into an individual's job, cross-functional learning, creating new challenges for individuals, asking workers to adapt quickly, and requiring the use of computer technology. Necessary steps in building these jobs include designing job accountability, giving decision-making authority to a team, defining a realistic job preview, acclimating employees to the new job, and providing feedback, as well as addressing the appropriate method for compensation. Virtual teams also need to design interaction with stakeholders so that team members have access to information from supervisors and so that supervisors are frequently aware of what team members are doing. Assigning a "team liaison" role may meet this need. Coordinating work with technology goes beyond understanding what tools are available to also understanding what tools appropriately meet the needs of the task. Finally, upon reentry or transition to a new project, team members need to alert managers of their availability and their skills, and supervisors need specific plans for enabling an efficient transition. A series of checklists outlines actions managers can take to accomplish these important determinants to successful virtual teamwork.

***

Graetz, K. A., Boyle, E. S., Kimble, C. E., Thompson, P., & Garloch, J. L. (1998). Information sharing in face-to-face, teleconferencing, and electronic chat teams. *Small Group Research, 29,* 714-743.

In this laboratory study, researchers sought to determine the impact of different communication channels (face-to-face, audio teleconferencing, and electronic chat) on effectiveness in completing a task (including performance, time to decision, perceived workload, and impressions of the group). One hundred forty-eight students were divided into thirty-seven teams, each using one of the three communications channels. Each group member held different pieces of information that were necessary to correctly complete the task, and each group had to combine information to arrive at the solution. Teams using the electronic chat format were significantly less accurate in their performance than either the face-to-face or the teleconferencing teams; they took longer to reach their decision, and they perceived their workload to be significantly higher. Additionally, group members using the electronic chat format indicated that they were less motivated to do the task and were less likely to believe that others in the group accurately portrayed information. These results demonstrated that performance on a task is related to the communication medium chosen to do the task.

***

Grenier, R., & Metes, G. (1995). *Going virtual: Moving your organization into the 21st century.* Upper Saddle River, NJ: Prentice-Hall, 320 pages.

Using organizational case studies, these authors discussed knowledge worker and stakeholder involvement issues in virtual operations. The authors also examined technology; organizational considerations during the move toward virtual operations; and processes for designing virtual work tasks, communications, and virtual teams. In Chapter 10, Virtual Teaming, the authors outlined the fundamental distinctions between GDTs and CLTs and laid out the benefits of virtual collaboration, including a variety of ways to maximize the use of distributed human and non-human resources. Following the case study of a multi-organizational team preparing a proposal, the authors outlined general and specific barriers to virtual teaming. For companies designing GDTs, they recommended observing decision-making processes and assessing competencies, skill requirements, current teaming practices, and attitudes toward changes. The authors also suggested concentrating on empowering the team and stakeholders and offered insights on managing morale, recognition, and rewards. Chapter 20, Designing Virtual Teaming, expands on these guidelines with a series of activities and strategies directed toward answering key questions regarding necessary competencies, team profiles, team environment and barriers, information access, the decision-making process, measurement and rewards, and stakeholder and team empowerment.

***

Hallowell, E. M. (1999, January-February). The human moment at work. *Harvard Business Review,* pp. 58-66.

The objective of this article was to remind readers that although "high tech" is efficient, relying too heavily on technology to communicate leads to a loss of true human contact. Loss of human contact in turn leads to confusion, alienation, isolation, and high levels of anxiety (or toxic worry). The author reminded readers that the "human moment," which he defined as an authentic psychological encounter that requires people's physical presence and their emotional and intellectual attention, is crucial to healthy human functioning.

***

Handy, C. (1995, May-June). Trust and the virtual organization. *Harvard Business Review*, pp. 40-50.

This article examined the managerial dilemmas that "virtuality" brings to an organization or team. The author identified trust as the biggest challenge and presented "seven cardinal principles" of trust: (1) Trust is not blind. It is unwise to trust people whom you do not know well, whom you have not observed in action over time, and who are not committed to the same goals. (2) Trust needs boundaries. Unlimited trust is, in practice, unrealistic. By *trust*, organizations really mean confidence in someone's competence and in his or her commitment to a goal. Define that goal, and the individual or the team can be trusted to complete it. Freedom within boundaries works best, however, when the work unit is self-contained and has the capability within it to solve its own problems. (3) Trust demands learning. A necessary condition of constancy is an ability to change; teams must always be flexible enough to change when times and customers demand it. Every individual on the team has to be capable of self-renewal. (4) Trust is tough. Trust has to be ruthless. When trust proves to be misplaced—not because people are deceitful or malicious but because they do not live up to expectations or cannot be relied on to do what is needed—then those who abrogated their responsibilities must go. It is because trust is so important, but so risky, that organizations tend to restrict their core commitments to a smaller group of what the author called "trusties." (5) Trust needs bonding. For the whole to work, the goals of the smaller units have to gel with the goals of the whole. In addition to using vision and mission statements, the executive leadership must communicate by personal example. (6) Trust needs touch. A shared commitment still requires personal contact to make it real. The more virtual an organization becomes, the more its people need to meet in person. (7) Trust requires leaders. When at their best, the units in trust-based organizations hardly have to be managed, but they do need several leaders. The author used the example of the multiple leaders in a rowing crew to support his thesis that all the leadership requirements of a virtual organization or team cannot be discharged by one person, no matter how great or how good the individual is.

***

Haywood, M. (1998). *Managing virtual teams: Practical techniques for high-technology project managers.* Boston: Artech House Publishers, 210 pages.

This book, based on survey data and the author's own experiences, is a practical guide for managers who are developing and leading GDTs. The author outlined the advantages and challenges of GDTs, then discussed communicating within the team, building the team, and managing and organizing the team remotely. The book also touched on such topics as networking technology and implementing telecommuting. Advantages of GDTs included access to a less-expensive labor pool, reduced office space, greater utilization of employees, a round-the-clock workforce, greater access to technical experts, a larger pool of possible job candidates (and conversely a larger pool of jobs to choose from), increased independence, greater flexibility, and opportunity for travel. Challenges included more difficult team building, cultural issues, the cost and complexity of technology, process and workflow, communication, technical support, recognition, inclusion versus isolation, and management resistance.

In terms of communication, the author pointed out how the control of information shifts when comparing communication in a GDT to communication in traditional teams. In a typical face-to-face meeting, the person transmitting the information has control. However, when communicating along technological channels in an asynchronous manner, the person receiving the information has control. This shift in communication patterns has a big impact on group processes. The author used models, lists, and her own experience to outline issues for consideration and to construct how-to steps for managers building GDTs.

***

Hedlund, J., Ilgen, D. R., & Hollenbeck, J. R. (1998). Decision accuracy in computer-mediated versus face-to-face decision-making teams. *Organizational Behavior and Human Decision Processes, 76,* 30-47.

   The research reported in this paper tested five hypotheses: (1) Team members communicating face-to-face are better informed regarding the information held by other team members than those communicating through computer mediation. (2) Team members communicating face-to-face will make more valid recommendations to their leader than those communicating through computer mediation. (3) Team leaders in computer-mediated conditions are more sensitive to the individual making valid recommendations in the team than those meeting face-to-face (called *hierarchical sensitivity*). (4) The degree to which team members remain informed, staff validity, and hierarchical sensitivity mediate the effect communication modes have on decision accuracy. (5) When hierarchical sensitivity is controlled, CLTs have an advantage over computer-mediated communication.

   To test these hypotheses, 256 undergraduate students were divided into sixty-four teams (thirty-two teams communicated by computer and thirty-two teams met face-to-face). The task was designed so that there was a correct answer, but individual team members did not hold all the information needed to reach the correct decision and so were compelled to communicate. Each team member separately submitted recommendations to the team leader. Results showed that, as hypothesized, CLT members were better informed and their teams had stronger staff validity, while GDTs had higher hierarchical sensitivity. Informal teams, staff validity, and hierarchical sensitivity did mediate the relationship between communication medium and performance. Finally, the performance advantage of CLTs over GDTs became greater when hierarchical sensitivity was held constant.

***

Henry, J. E., & Hartzler, M. (1997). Virtual teams: Today's reality, today's challenge. *Quality Progress, 30*(5), 108-109.

   This article characterized what GDTs are, how they operate, and what benefits they provide, and described how organizations can make GDTs work. According to the article, GDT members are mutually accountable for team results and solve problems and make decisions jointly. Additionally, geographical dispersion forces GDT members to use whatever means exist to stay in contact with one another so the job gets done. GDTs are beneficial, argued the authors, because anyone can be on the GDT team (as long as there is an available link), there is a degree of anonymity among members, and team members can share databases. To make GDTs work, team members should meet face-to-face for the start-up session. It is necessary to develop and plan what the team intends to do and how it will accomplish its goals. Members need to be trained regarding the technological methodologies and software necessary to work together over a distance. Organizations must make teams a top priority and hold them responsible for their objectives. GDTs must also deal with the human element, allowing personal contact and informal social time among members. Finally, organizations must remember that team building is iterative—not a one-shot deal.

***

Hightower, R., & Hagmann, C. (1995). Social influence effects on remote group interactions. *Journal of International Information Management, 4,* 17-32.

   This research study investigated the differences between CLTs and GDTs in patterns of social influence and the outcomes of those patterns, particularly as information load increases. It was hypothesized that CLTs would primarily use informational influence (carefully constructed arguments or the transmission of large volumes of information) while GDTs would predominantly use normative influence (emotional arguments and statements of preference) when completing a group decision-making task. Furthermore, it was thought that as information load increases, CLTs' use of informational influence would increase and their use of normative influence would decrease. Finally, it was also hypothesized that GDTs would exhibit less shifting among choices than CLTs. To test these hypotheses, eleven CLTs and thirteen GDTs (which used an electronic meeting system) were studied as they performed a decision-making task. The group interactions were coded according to informational and normative influence definition, and individual pre- and post-discussion decision confidence was used to evaluate the degree to which the team shifted among choices. Analysis found that CLTs do use more informational influence, particularly under conditions of high information load; these teams also display more shifting choices under high information load. GDTs did not use significantly more normative influence.

***

Hightower, R., & Sayeed, L. (1994). The impact of computer mediated communication systems on biased group discussion. *Computers in Human Behavior, 11,* 33-44.

   This study investigated the degree to which information load and the distribution of information among group members affect the frequency of biased discussion in teams performing a candidate selection task. Although teams may make better decisions than individuals because they bring a larger amount of information to the decision task, the load of information that the group has to manage and the extent to which members share the same information may lead to discussion biased toward that shared information and away from information that is not shared. An experiment with ninety-three undergraduate students separated into fifteen face-to-face teams and sixteen computer-mediated teams tested these hypotheses. The authors also hypothesized that computer-mediated teams will experience more biased discussion than face-to-face teams, particularly in conditions of high information load and high information distribution. Information load was manipulated by giving several teams five additional candidate attributes for consideration. Information distribution was manipulated by providing one condition with 60 percent shared information and the other condition with 33 percent shared information. The degree of biased discussion was calculated by combining the number of positive and negative attributes accorded to the candidates in a pre-test and a post-test (discussion). Biased discussion was more frequent in computer-mediated teams, under conditions of high shared information, and in conditions of high information load for computer-mediated teams only. The authors suggested that as tasks become more complex and equivocal, computer-mediated groupwork is more subject to discussion biases.

✳✳✳

Hinds, P., & Kiesler, S. (1995). Communication across boundaries: Work, structure, and use of communication technologies in a large organization. *Organization Science, 6,* 373-393.

   To understand how different types of workers communicate, logs of communication over two days from seven departments in a telecommunications company were examined for degree of lateral, vertical, diagonal, inside/outside chain-of-command, and intra- and extradepartmental communication, and for use of several technologies (for example, telephone, voice mail, e-mail). The authors hypothesized that technical employees would communicate laterally and use the telephone and e-mail more than administrative employees. In addition, it was predicted that all employees would use the telephone for lateral communication and for communication outside the chain of command and outside the department. Findings showed that although technical employees had more lateral communications, most lateral communication was by telephone. Technical employees used e-mail, but administrators used voice mail. Surprisingly, much of the total communication was extradepartmental. The differences in communication patterns between technical and administrative employees may be explained by the flatter structure of technical work teams. The differences in telephone, voice mail, and e-mail use may reflect the need for social context cues in various task situations.

***

Igbaria, M., & Tan, M. (Eds.). (1998). *The virtual workplace*. Hershey, PA: Idea Group Publishing, 416 pages.

The purpose of this edited book is to discuss the concepts of the virtual workplace, what is driving this phenomenon, and its consequences. The chapters are drawn from a variety of disciplines and consider a variety of scenarios. Although this book deals primarily with organizations, GDT issues arise throughout. The first of the book's four sections deals with issues and benefits of virtual organizations. General conclusions stated that virtual organizations use technology differently than organizations using GDTs. Virtual organizations rely more on the World Wide Web and less on groupware or e-mail. Also, GDTs can collaborate on complex tasks and socialize without meeting face-to-face. Critical success factors for GDTs include an infrastructure and culture that support this type of interaction, and adequate levels of trust and openness. The book's second section dealt with applications and covered such topics as distance training, workflow management systems, "virtual consultants," use of technology in cities, simulations, and use of collaborative notebooks. One study in this section showed that ad hoc GDTs exchange information less effectively than ad hoc CLTs, but that ongoing GDTs exchange information more effectively than ongoing CLTs.

The third section dealt with telecommuting and remote work, addressing such topics as balancing work and family life, the economic costs and benefits of telecommuting, distance education, combining knowledge about telecommuting and GDTs, and creating a mobile workforce. The final section dealt with human issues such as unions and group development. Using a case study, authors demonstrated that GDTs also go through the forming, storming, norming, performing, and adjourning stages of group development. Additionally, writers surmised that e-mail gives groups the illusion of physical and emotional closeness.

***

James, G. (1998). *Success secrets from Silicon Valley: How to make your teams more effective no matter what business you're in*. New York: Random House, 384 pages.

James looked at phenomenally successful companies in Silicon Valley to determine how they work, and drew eight practices common to those companies: (1) they view business as an ecosystem, not a battlefield; (2) they see corporations as communities, not as machines; (3) they view management as a service mechanism, not a control mechanism; (4) they accept employees as peers, not as children; (5) they motivate through vision, not fear; (6) they perceive change as growth, not pain; (7) they use computers as servants, not masters; and (8) they transform work into play.

The practice of most relevance to the topic of GDTs focuses on using computers as servants, not masters. When used as a master, technology can separate employees from one other and measure productivity by numbers (for example, the number of screens that employees can process during a work-day). Viewed as a servant, technology can provide flexibility to employees in terms of where, when, and how they work.

***

Jarvenpaa, S. L., Knoll, K., & Leidner, D. E. (1998). Is anybody out there? Antecedents of trust in global virtual teams. *Journal of Management Information Systems, 14*(4), 29-64.

The focus of this research study was to explore the antecedents of trust in global GDTs. Seventy-five teams of four to six graduate students participating in a global virtual collaboration course (a total of 385 partici-pants from twenty-eight universities around the world) were used in this study. The researchers tested hypotheses regarding the development of trust in global GDTs that communicated solely through electronic means and never met face-to-face. The teams worked on three projects; two were team devel-opment projects and one was the final project. Quantitative results showed that an individual's propensity to trust had a positive effect on an individual's overall trust in the team. Team-building exercises also had a positive effect on the perceptions of other members' integrity, ability, and benevolence but did not have a direct effect on trust itself. In early phases of the teamwork, trust was predicted more strongly by perceptions of other team members' integrity and ability but not on their perceived benevolence. Over time, benevolence gained a positive influence on trust while the influence of ability lessened. Qualitative results suggest that high-trust teams exhibited trust behaviors from the very beginning of the interactions (the researchers call this "swift trust") and took an action orientation, as compared to low trust teams.

***

Jessup, L. M., & Valacich, J. S. (Eds.). (1993). *Group support systems: New perspectives*. New York: Macmillan.

This edited volume presented readings on a number of interrelated group support systems (GSS) issues, providing the readers (researchers, graduate students, and practitioners) with a foundation of GSS research. Although the readings were limited to those teams meeting in a same-time, same-place environment, many of the lessons can be applied to GDTs. The book's four sections included an overview of GSS; research issues; design, development, and use issues; and bridging GSS to other disciplines. The book opened with the suggestion that GSS, like many innovations, not only change how people act and perform, but also radically alter the way they think about the world. The works collected in this volume suggested that GSS have capacity not only to improve group work but also to change the notions of what it means to work in a group.

The book's overview section listed GSS research facilities and the type of research being conducted. The second section discussed research, theory, and methodology issues. In terms of research, the editors concluded that the effects of GSS depend on a variety of factors, including technology, group, and task. They suggested that larger teams benefited more from GSS than smaller teams, that GSS were more suitable for complex tasks than simple tasks, and that GSS were more beneficial for generation tasks and less helpful for choice tasks. GSS increased anonymity, but the effects of this on performance were mixed. GSS also allowed the group members to work in parallel, which had a positive impact on performance. Finally, GSS changed the structure of group interaction, improving performance when such interaction fit the task but decreasing performance when interaction did not match the task.

In terms of theory, the book's chapters approached GSS from two perspectives. The first perspective, the more common approach, assumed that the organization is an assembly of individuals and that GSS are instruments for democracy and gain. The second approach was collectivist, assuming that organizations are social structures and that, therefore, GSS are evolutionary products. These two perspectives provided the basis for theories in decision-making, group process, and communication (institutional and coordination). However, the theories were missing important elements, such as dealing with affective aspects, morals, diversity, and freedom and power. The chapter on methodology makes six recommendations for future research: (1) share measurement information, (2) provide measurement information, (3) triangulate, (4) continue lab studies but increase field studies, (5) study longitudinally, and (6) increase the depth of qualitative analyses.

The book's third section outlined the importance of support and infrastructure for teams using technology. Such teams need technology and facilitation skills, and facilities and interfaces need to be designed for maximum benefit. It appeared, from the writings, that technology can help teams by allowing parallel communications, anonymity, group memory, process structures, and task support. These processes may have a positive impact in some cases but may be detrimental in aiding teams in sense-making activities. The book's final section questioned how GSS affect the nature of the organization and its decisions, behavioral decision theory, communication theory, and computer-assisted learning.

***

Johansen, R., Sibbet, D., Senson, S., Martin, A., Mittman, R., & Saffo, P. (1991). *Leading business teams: How teams can use technology and group process tools to enhance performance*. New York: Addison-Wesley, 216 pages.

This book discussed *groupware*: what it is, why it is needed, what tools are included, and how to use it to make teams more effective. The authors began this practical guide, assembled from quantitative and qualitative field research results, by describing two models that they used as a context for discussing groupware. The first model addressed time and place, and the second model addressed team development. Conceptually, teams can meet in four ways. They can hold same-time, same-place meetings (face-to-face meetings are so ubiquitous that they are not often considered technology or groupware, but the authors argued that they are). Teams can also meet at the same time but in different places, at different times but in the same place, and at different times in different places. The authors diverged here from much of the present literature, suggesting that teams do not need to use the same "meeting" technologies each time but should instead choose one based on their stage of development. The authors used Drexler, Sibbet, and Forrester (1988; see reference list) to discuss the development of team performance: orientation, trust building, goal and role clarification, commitment, implementation, high performance, and renewal. They suggested that teams that are getting oriented and building trust should use same-time, same-place technology. When clarifying and committing, teams should operate in the same time. During implementation and high performance, teams can be in different times. During renewal, teams again need to meet face-to-face.

The authors also identified three pockets into which much of the current groupware technology can be put: the telephone, the computer, and the conference room (or some combination of the three). The authors also discussed the costs, pitfalls, and benefits of groupware. Costs include setting up the initial system, additional staffing needs that accompany new system installation, and maintenance and growth of the system. The pitfalls include basic human nature, trying to use the new technology to solve everything, using technology incorrectly or haphazardly (without trying to connect the systems), and trying to use the wrong technology at the wrong time. The authors argued that, when used well, groupware can achieve cost reductions and other benefits. It can also have unconventional influences, such as altering how the group or even the organization works. In conclusion, the authors made recommendations on ensuring group effectiveness, including training teams to use the technology, paying attention to the group and group dynamics, planning meetings, and watching for problems.

***

Kimball, L. (1995). Ten ways to make online learning groups work. *Educational Leadership, 53*(2), 54-56.

To enhance the on-line experience of visitors to virtual learning communities, this article suggested ten actions: (1) identifying a purpose, (2) defining roles, (3) creating an atmosphere unique to the group, (4) nourishing conversation, (5) acknowledging contributors privately and publicly, (6) adjusting the pace so all members feel up-to-date, (7) supporting and recruiting new members, (8) synthesizing the group's collective responses, (9) tracking the participation of the various members, and (10) staying aware of what the group is doing rather than harping on what it should be doing.

***

Kiser, K. (1999, March). Working on world time. *Training, 33*(3), 28-34.

This article discussed existing trends for members of virtual teams, as reported by researchers who serve on virtual teams. The author also described the variety of training and consultation provided by experts within various corporations and within virtual team and information consulting firms. Virtual teams currently consist of members working blocks apart or thousands of miles apart and include representatives from a single or multiple organizations. Jessica Lipnack (see Lipnack & Stamps, 1997) suggested that most people will do at least some of their work this way. While executives may see virtual teams as both a selling point for recruiting and a vehicle for obtaining the best skills for a project regardless of where the employee with those skills is located, Lipnack and Deborah Duarte (see Duarte & Snyder, 1999) believed that virtual teams may struggle because of lack of purpose, poor leadership, miscommunication, technical glitches, and cultural differences. With the help of consultants, some companies like Nortel have created advisory Web sites, and others like Shell Oil have created formal training programs to enhance managers' abilities to communicate with remote team members, hold effective meetings, and communicate across cultures. Duarte and Nancy Snyder (1999) suggested, however, that more attention be paid to simulations, in which team members practice leading a virtual team through simulated meetings and agenda planning.

***

Kling, R. (1996). Social relationships in electronic forums. Hangouts, salons, workplace and communities. In R. Kling (Ed.), *Computerization and controversy: Value conflicts and social choices* (2nd ed., pp. 426-453). San Diego, CA: Academic Press, 961 pages.

This chapter examined specific controversies about the kinds of social relations that people develop when they communicate via computer networks. According to the author, the way that people work and communicate by computer networks destabilizes many conventional social categories. While this chapter did not specifically mention GDTs, it offered an interesting perspective on how technology affects work life.

***

Kossler, M. E., & Prestridge, S. (1996). Geographically dispersed teams. *Issues & Observations, 16*(2/3), 9-11.

With a simple introductory scenario, the authors showed how complicated the normally straightforward task of planning a meeting can be when working with a GDT. This article also stated a number of issues that GDTs face that are different from issues faced by CLTs: greater effort is necessary to align group members around a shared commitment to team goals; more time is required to build trust among group members; it is more difficult to establish and maintain roles and responsibilities and to mesh the various practices members bring with them; it is harder to identify and resolve miscommunication; it is harder to contend with various field-office cultures; and more effort is needed to address and resolve conflicts, which can easily go unidentified. The authors explored six strategies to deal with these issues: (1) hold an initial face-to-face start-up meeting to build a socialization process, (2) establish a high level of interdependency among team members by creating shared visions and selecting members with complementary skills, (3) establish a schedule of regular communication and face-to-face meetings for permanent GDTs, (4) set norms for sharing information and responding to messages and for surfacing and resolving conflicts, (5) encourage the development of relationships, and (6) recognize and honor diversity of culture (beyond the influence of work styles) by encouraging the sharing of culture.

***

Kostner, J. (1994). *Virtual leadership: Secrets from the Round Table for the multi-site manager*. New York: Time-Warner Books, 174 pages.

In this "business novel," Kostner used the story of King Arthur and the Round Table to discuss strategies for developing a multi-site team. These strategies take the form of key symbols from the legend of King Arthur. Because most distant team members tend not to know each other well, have few traditional opportunities to get to know each other, and communicate poorly across distance, trust becomes an issue. Excalibur, a symbol of leadership, represents the virtual leader's critical role and most difficult challenge: building trust. The Round Table itself symbolizes unity and the need for distant members to see themselves as a team. Because virtual work teams typically lose traditional forums for sharing information equally and effectively, the author used the joust to symbolize how the virtual team leader finds ways to solve problems. Vision, mission, and goals are important to all teams because they provide the emotional and intellectual commitment that helps bind individuals together—Camelot serves as the symbol. Lancelot serves as a reminder that the unique needs of all members must be attended to by the leader. Finally, with distributed teams, members in various sites tend to receive and create different information and have different contexts for interpreting information. In the author's work, Merlin symbolizes how to communicate effectively across distance.

***

Kraut, R., Galegher, J., Fish, R., & Chalfonte, B. (1992). Task requirements and media choice in collaborative writing. *Human-Computer Interaction, 7*, 375-407.

This article outlined an interview study and three experiments that addressed the choices authors make for collaborative writing, the fit between task and technology required for collaborative writing tasks, and the problems associated with writing that uses technological tools for mediation. Media richness theory, which serves as the starting point for this research, states that tasks of greater uncertainty require "richer" media to enable better communication and mediation. According to the authors' expanded theory, structural contingency theory, media also have interactive components (capable of exchanging information rapidly and adjusting messages to the responses of collaborators) and expressive components (capable of conveying the intensity and subtleties of meaning through paralanguage and nonverbal gestures).

Through interviews with fifty-five individuals from writing teams, the authors concluded that collaborators need substantial face-to-face communication at the highly equivocal planning phases. Experiments with student participants also showed that collaborators often choose rich media for planning and revising work while using leaner media for draft writing. When students in another experiment were prevented from using the media of their choice, those who worked with lean media, such as computer conferencing, had greater difficulty achieving consensus, coordinating activities, and communicating about content. In a final experiment, the authors compared the effect of using voice mail or written messages when participants provided draft annotations to others' work. Those using voice messages more often commented on global problems in a draft. Recipients judged voiced comments to be better, more useful, more complete, and to contain more explanation and justification. This last experiment demonstrated the importance of the expressive richness of media, in this case voice over text, to transmit complex meaning.

***

Lally, R., & Kostner, J. (1997). Learn to be a distance manager. *Getting Results, 42*(7), 6-7.

In this paper, the authors discussed three problems that can occur in GDTs: nonresponsiveness, location-centric words and actions, and lack of "water cooler" time. The authors suggested that leaders must remain in close contact with all the GDT members without overusing "cyber-junk mail," keep team members focused, allow informal time for GDT members to get together (even if not face-to-face), and take into account the special needs of members located off-site (give them interesting assignments, do not refer to them as "those people," and schedule meetings at convenient times).

***

Lea, M., & Spears, R. (1992). Paralanguage and social perception in computer-mediated communication. *Journal of Organizational Computing, 2*(3&4), 321-341.

This article argued against the concept that computer-mediated communication frees group members from interpersonal and normative factors that form a social context and influences the way they interact. According to many researchers, computer-mediated communication can remove visual and auditory cues, de-individuating group members and resulting in more honesty and less posturing in group interaction. This article suggested that communicators create a social context in all situations, forming impressions of others based on group identity or paralanguage (linguistics or writing style) cues if auditory and visual cues are unavailable. Thus, computer-mediated communication cannot eliminate social context.

To test this hypothesis in a group environment, the authors conducted two experiments in which participants were asked to evaluate the personal attributes of other (seen/unseen) group members, based on the information received through computer mediation. In the first experiment, novice e-mail users (twenty-four undergraduates) and experienced e-mail users (twenty-four technical employees from a telecommunications company) were asked about the impressions they formed of authors of various e-mail messages that contained experimentally manipulated spelling and typing errors. In the second experiment, group influence was manipulated by telling some of the forty-eight undergraduate participants, randomly assigned to groups of three, that they should act as a group, while others were told to act as individuals. Results suggested that both novice and experienced e-mail users employ paralanguage cues to gather social information, and that the meaning attached to paralanguage cues depends on whether or not a group or an individual context is emphasized. When physically isolated, group members in an individualistic context view their communicators as more negative, while a group context facilitates more positive evaluations. These results suggested that computer-mediated communication may not be as neutral as previously thought.

***

Lipnack, J., & Stamps, J. (1997). *Virtual teams: Reaching across space, time, and organizations with technology.* New York: John Wiley, 256 pages.

Virtual Teams is the final book in a trilogy about networked organizations that the authors have been writing since 1991. The focus of the book fell on small teams of people working across boundaries and supported by computer and communications technologies; it highlighted the human side of the organization-technology relationship. The authors first defined virtual teams, gave some examples of how companies use them (both low- and high-tech versions), and then provided broad answers to the question, "Why virtual teams?" Detailed case studies of six companies and related GDTs were scattered throughout the book. Each chapter ended with an integrated framework for understanding and managing virtual teams, and the book closed with tools and methods necessary for starting and maintaining GDTs.

***

Lloyd, P. (1994). *Groupware in the 21st century: Computer-supported cooperative working toward the millennium.* Westport, CT: Praeger, 336 pages.

This book presents a nontechnical view of the future of information technology and group processes. The author discussed the current state of technology and its origins; described the tools and technologies that are being used to support teams; and discussed the "likely" impact on organizations, teams, and creativity. Finally, he presented a range of possible future scenarios.

For the purposes of this report, part four of the book, the impact of groupware on teams, is most relevant. Conclusions suggested that there is a real need for computer-supported cooperative work (CSCW) tools. This sort of technology aids decision-making by capturing large amounts of information in a single location, aids in complex analyses, and enables teams to communicate from different places at different times. But for CSCW tools to realize their potential, both the design of the system and its implementation must reflect organizational needs. In turn, the organization must be flexible and creative in using the system to its fullest benefit. Additionally, individuals need to be developed and rewarded for relying on teams and CSCW to do their work.

***

Mankin, D., Cohen, S. G., & Bikson, T. K. (1996). *Teams and technology: Fulfilling the promise of the new organization.* Boston: Harvard Business School Press, 284 pages.

This book discussed how to develop and integrate teams, information technology, and high-level policies and structures to create more effective organizations. The authors introduced the mutual design and implementation framework as a perspective for understanding and addressing many of the key issues currently facing organizations. The authors never specifically mention GDTs, but they do offer insights into the types of organization-wide changes necessary to support user teams and new technologies. They also speculated about the team-based, technology-enabled organization of the future.

***

Marucca, R. F. (1998, July-August). How do you manage an off-site team? *Harvard Business Review,* pp. 22-26.

This case study described a department whose employees previously worked in a CLT manner but then switched to more flexible working arrangements that allowed them to work off-site. Although the head of the department thinks the team is "doing the best work they have ever done," he also realizes that the virtual relationships are fraught with personal problems that are difficult to resolve using electronic media (e-mail, for example). The manager feels disconnected from his subordinates because he cannot see them doing their work or see them interacting with each other in their work, even though he is more "connected" to them than he has ever been before. This case study pointed out a common dilemma managers face with GDTs: managing people they cannot see.

***

McGrath, J. E., & Berdahl, J. L. (1998). Groups, technology, and time: Use of computers for collaborative work. In R. S. Tinsdale, L. Heath, J. Edwards, F. J. Posavac, F. B. Bryant, Y. Suarez-Balacazar, E. Henderson-King, & J. Myers (Eds.), *Theory and research on small groups* (pp. 205-228). New York: Plenum Press, 300 pages.

This book chapter described two longitudinal studies addressing the team use of electronic technology over time. The main research question addressed in both studies was how group process, task performance, and participant reactions vary as a function of the group's membership composition, its communication technology, and the type of task the group is working on; and how these relations change over time. Both studies used teams of students participating in classes where they were expected, as one of the course requirements, to work in teams. The first study included eighty students in twenty-two teams. The second study had 119 students, but the authors did not mention how many teams. The teams were studied in a variety of ways throughout the semester. In terms of performance, CLTs performed better on written group essays than did GDTs in the first two weeks, but by the third week that difference had disappeared. This suggested that any performance differences between the two mediums (face-to-face and dispersed) may be due to the newness of the computer-mediated interaction rather than to specific problems in GDTs. Additionally, in the first study, one person from each CLT and one person from each GDT was responsible for writing the final essay (all team members had input). When the GDTs were given the technology to write the essay as a group, they were able to consistently outperform CLTs. In terms of interactions, GDTs began with and continued to have higher levels of task activity and lower levels of social activity than CLTs. Additionally, the dispersed-group members were less positive about their teams.

At the end of the chapter, the authors offered three implications about group work and technology. First, technology is ubiquitous, both driving and constraining group action. (Technology was defined as any set of tools, rules, procedures, and resources that the group uses, including face-to-face meetings.) Therefore, it is necessary to understand differences when teams change technology, not when they get technology. Second, technology effects are interaction effects; that is, technology by itself does not impact the group, but the way technology interacts with the group situation impacts the group and the group outcomes (such as how well the technology fits the task and how well the task, the technology, and the group membership fit together). Third, teams are dynamic systems that change over time. Time is both a vehicle for the accrual of experience and a vehicle for the impact of change. Accrual of experience brings about changes in how the group works together. The impact of change includes changes in membership, changes in the projects the group is working on, changes in the technology available, and changes to the context of the situation. These two vehicles, experience accrual and impact of change, are different, but interact.

***

McGrath, J. E., & Hollingshead, A. B. (1994). *Groups interacting with technology: Ideas, evidence, issues and an agenda*. Thousand Oaks, CA: Sage Publications, 192 pages.

These authors and their colleagues have been at the forefront of the effort to provide a framework for empirical study of technology-assisted groupwork. This book argued for a more complex understanding of how teams work with technology. The authors classified the main areas in which technology can assist a group in developing group communication support systems (GCSS), group information support systems (GISS), group external communication support systems (GXSS), and group performance support systems (GPSS).

The authors summarized proposed conceptual formulations. From research on GPSS, Nunamaker and colleagues (Nunamaker et al., 1996) at the University of Arizona argue that technology can contribute to "process gains" through process structure and support and through outcome structure and support of group decision-making tasks. DeSanctis and colleagues (DeSanctis & Poole, 1994) at the University of Minnesota applied adaptive structuration theory to group processes to explain how a group adapts technology and its procedures into a set of social practices. The report also summarizes the concepts of social presence, information richness, and the interaction among time, tasks, and technology (based on the authors' time, interaction, and performance theory).

The authors also summarized empirical results across a variety of studies on teams interacting with technology. Some of the findings included: the volume of participation among group members is smaller but more equally distributed than in conventional teams; computer-mediated teams take longer to complete their tasks and are less likely to achieve consensus, but if they do, their degree of consensus is higher; and teams using technology produce higher-quality products for idea generation (brainstorming) but lower-quality products for intellective and negotiation tasks. Most of the single-meeting studies summarized in the report do not consider the impact of group size, composition, structure, time and space dispersion, or task types.

Finally, the report presented a conceptual framework composed of input variables (for example, member and group attributes, tasks/projects/purposes, technology, and context factors—all of which interact), organizing concepts, process variables, and outcome factors (for example, task performance effectiveness, user reactions, and member relations). To conclude, the authors presented a number of themes for future research, including multiple criteria for assessment, variations in member and group characteristics, variations in task and technology factors, and the impact of changes over time and the interactions that may exist with the passage of time. An extensive annotated bibliography of research conducted prior to 1994 was also included.

***

McLeod, P. L., Baron, R. S., Marti, M. W., & Yoon, K. (1997). The eyes have it: Minority influence in face-to-face and computer-mediated group discussion. *Journal of Applied Psychology, 82,* 706-718.

This article considered two aspects of minority opinions in group decision-making (the expression of minority opinions and the influence of those opinions) and their impact on face-to-face discussions, and two dispersed conditions: anonymous and non-anonymous (in both of these conditions, participants could see each other, but they could only communicate using technology). Minorities were defined as holding a different opinion than a majority of the other group members. Fifty-nine four-person teams made up of 236 undergraduate and graduate students participated in the study. One person in each group was randomly designated as a minority and received different information about a problem than the other three members. The research demonstrated that minority opinion holders expressed their arguments most frequently under anonymous conditions using technology; however, the influence of the minority arguments was highest in face-to-face discussion.

***

Melymuka, K. (1997). Virtual realities. *ComputerWorld, 31*(17), 70-73.

The author asserted that "virtual teams are counterintuitive, difficult to design, costly, and complex to implement, messy to manage, and far less productive that 'real' teams." But in the current work environment, the article continued, they are necessary. The author offered suggestions: the corporate culture must support teams; team members need to have good verbal, listening, and writing skills; time needs to be coordinated so that members in one time zone do not have to depend on those in other time zones to complete tasks; decisions about which interactions can occur as synchronous and which as asynchronous must be made; technology needs to be similar across sites; team members must be comfortable using the technology; workloads need to be managed because when people are dispersed, it is harder to judge responsibilities; network and system support during every member's working hours must be available; and cultural differences and differences in communication styles need to be understood, planned for, and managed.

***

Mustaler, L. (1995, November/December). Effective teamwork virtually guaranteed. *Network World Collaboration (Supplement), 12*(42), 10-11.

The author shared personal examples of the pitfalls that exist for GDTs. Although GDTs enhance flexibility by pulling together the resources appropriate for the project no matter where those resources are, managers must assemble people with complementary skill sets, philosophies, and task orientations. The people selected for this teamwork need to be highly motivated and self-directed because geographical dispersion limits direct supervision. Performance evaluation can be difficult for the same reasons. Establishing project objectives and giving a team the opportunity to bond are important activities when the team is forming. The author also suggested some technology considerations.

***

Nunamaker, J. F., Jr. (1997). Future research in group support systems: Needs, some questions and possible directions. *International Journal of Human–Computer Studies, 47,* 357-385.

In this article, Nunamaker discussed the future of group support systems (GSS) research in terms of what is needed, outlined important research questions, and offered some possible future directions. GSS is a set of techniques, software, and technology designed to focus and enhance team communication, deliberations, and decision-making. Despite there being over two decades of research on GSS, few users employ such systems. One possibility for such reluctance is that GSS still requires users to change their own behavior rather than fitting itself smoothly into the group's decision-making process. To make GSS more attractive, Nunamaker believed several major issues need to be addressed: systems must be easy to learn; simply providing connectivity and data-sharing capabilities is insufficient—users must be taught how to work in a distributed mode; a means of representing a distributed environment (for example, using virtual reality) must be found; a way of improving facilitation in a GSS environment must be found; systems have to be designed to handle large quantities of information; and systems have to do a better job integrating technology into team operations.

***

Nunamaker, J. F., Jr., Briggs, R. O., Mittleman, D. D., Vogel, D. R., & Balthazard, P. A. (1996). Lessons learned from a dozen years of group support systems research: A discussion of lab and field findings. *Journal of Management Information Systems, 13,* 163-207.

The authors presented lessons drawn from group support systems (GSS) research, and built the foundation for a diagnostic tool for determining the appropriateness of various forms of groupware (GSS and e-mail, for example) for the coordination of individual and group tasks. Some of the lessons they discussed include: GSS technology does not replace leadership and does not imply any leadership style; GSS amplifies existing situations (for example, well-planned meetings become better and poorly planned meetings become worse); there must be incentives for individuals to contribute to group effort; GSS can dramatically reduce labor costs and project time; and GSS can also enhance meeting participation by increasing idea generation, energizing meeting participants, manipulating anonymity so ideas are evaluated more objectively and criticized constructively, and increasing participants' acceptance of the final outcome. Lessons relating to facilitation include: extensive pre-meeting planning and agenda setting is critical; a group must understand how activities move it toward its goal; new ideas will change the agenda; and alternating modes of interaction can prevent burnout. Other important lessons relate to cross-cultural and multicultural issues, designing GSS software, collaborative writing, electronic polling, facilities design, GSS in the classroom, and process reengineering.

***

Oakley, J. G. (1998). Leadership processes in virtual teams and organizations. *The Journal of Leadership Studies, 5*(3), 3-17.

In creating effective leadership processes, GDTs face different challenges than CLTs, yet little is known about those challenges. The objective of this article was to determine what they are. The author hypothesized that the role of top-level leaders is to change from a mindset of control to a mindset of trust. The role of top-level management is to provide an atmosphere within which a team can work. The leader of the team, whether assigned or chosen, needs to be an "empowered leader," that is, a leader with a democratic power orientation and a low level of involvement who exhibits such behaviors as self-regulation, boundary spanning, and resource gathering. Additionally, such leaders should concentrate on coordinating rather than directing team activities. They should design tasks to allow the maximum amount of individual and team discretion in decision-making. Finally, GDTs and their members need more "self leadership" and less top-down leadership.

* * *

Ocker, R., Hiltz, S. R., Turoff, M., & Fjermstad, J. (1995-1996). The effects of distributed group support and process structuring on software requirements of development teams: Results on creativity and quality. *Journal of Management Information Systems, 12*(3), 127-153.

When software development teams collaborate, more than half of the cost of development is attributable to the decisions made at the beginning stages of requirements definitions. For this reason, initial creative, innovative, and quality decisions are important. The authors of this article suggested that distributed asynchronous group interaction can be useful in this situation, but the lack of structure that may exist in distributed environments can limit creative processes. Working with theories of minority influence, group performance, and structured problem solving, the authors hypothesized that teams interacting only through a computer conferencing system (called EIES 2) would produce higher quality and more creative solutions than face-to-face teams, structured problem-solving teams would produce higher quality and more creative solutions than unstructured teams, and computer conferencing/ structured teams and face-to-face unstructured teams would produce higher quality and more creative solutions than computer conferencing/unstructured teams and face-to-face structured teams. Results from a study utilizing forty-one teams of 218 graduate students working on a design task found that while computer conferencing generally enhanced performance, structuring the problem-solving approach did not affect the outcome.

* * *

Odenwald, S. B. (1996). *Global solutions for teams: Moving from collision to collaboration.* Burr Ridge, IL: Irwin Professional Publishing, 195 pages.

This book's cultural guidelines and case examples of leading multinational corporations demonstrated how cross-cultural teams can overcome a disjointed state of cultural collision, progressing to the more productive stages of coexistence and, ultimately, collaboration. Odenwald, an authority on international management and training issues, drew from her personal experience to show how it is possible to implement productive cross-functional and cross-location teams, approach decisions and business challenges with an innate sense of "GlobalThink," and select and lead teams of individuals from diverse cultures in developing effective work systems.

***

O'Hara-Devereaux, M., & Johansen, R. (1994). *GlobalWork: Bridging distance, culture, and time.* San Francisco: Jossey-Bass, 439 pages.

Based on research conducted by the Institute for the Future on behalf of leading global organizations such as American Express, Apple Computer, and AT&T, the authors identified key competencies that managers need in order to succeed in a global workplace. The authors provided both sophisticated strategies and practical rules of thumb for a world in which agreements such as NAFTA are rapidly reshaping the global business environment and in which new information technologies are forcing organizations to redefine where, when, and how work is accomplished. This book addressed frustrating questions managers and line employees struggle with in the global workplace, such as: How do we build trust among team members, scattered all over the world, who have never met and probably never will? How do we implement a strategy for sharing information over half-a-dozen different national electronic infrastructures with widely varying quality? How do we motivate workers in Brazil and Japan to participate in a collaborative team with an African-American manager based in Los Angeles? How do we schedule a team conference call among members in Paris, New York, and Jakarta when working hours do not overlap? How does a team get things done on time when members have different concepts of time and different ideas about what it means to be "done"? How do we build and maintain a functioning culture in a strategic alliance or joint venture involving numerous functional, corporate, and national cultures, many of which clash with one another? *GlobalWork* was written both as a theoretical overview and a practical framework for bridging the chasms represented by cultures, distance, and time.

***

Olson, J. S., Olson, G. M., & Meader, D. (1997). Face-to-face group work compared to remote group work with and without video. In K. E. Finn, A. J. Sellen, & S. B. Wilbur (Eds.), *Video-mediated communication* (pp. 157-172). Mahwah, NJ: Lawrence Erlbaum Associates, 584 pages.

In this book chapter, the researchers described a study they conducted (using 222 MBA students in 74 three-person teams) comparing CLTs with GDTs. The CLTs used either a traditional whiteboard or a shared editor while GDTs used audio with the shared editor or video and audio with the shared editor. Dependent variables included group process, quality, and satisfaction measures. The researchers found that process differs between CLTs and GDTs. GDTs spend more time, on average, managing their work and clarifying what they mean than do CLTs. Regarding quality, CLTs using the shared editor performed better than GDTs using audio and the shared editor or CLTs using a whiteboard. There were no significant differences in quality between GDTs using video and the shared editor and either CLTs using the shared editor or GDTs using audio and the shared editor. This finding suggested that there is little difference in quality between CLTs and GDTs using video, and only a slight decrease in quality from GDTs using audio. However, group members were most satisfied with CLT meetings that used whiteboards. There was no difference in the satisfaction between CLTs using a shared editor and GDTs using video and a shared editor. Teams were least satisfied with GDTs using audio with their shared editor.

***

Oravec, J. A. (1996). *Virtual individuals, virtual groups: Human dimensions of groupware and computer networking.* Cambridge, England: Cambridge University Press, 389 pages.

The author argued that computing applications currently being used and developed are powerfully shaping and changing our culture, even though we may not be aware of it. Using anthropological theory on genres and artifacts, Oravec outlined why awareness of these changes is important. In the final chapter, Oravec made some suggestions regarding the best way to design collaborative-writing and group decision-making tools, both of which provide "vehicles for the construction of a group product." In making these suggestions, the author gave importance to the following questions: How does an individual's contributions or expressions appear to other group members, and how do the individual's contributions appear in relation to what is constructed as the "group product"? How are individuals and teams distributed in the organization? How are the forms and channels of interaction for group members structured, and are some members given limited access while others get special channels? What are the expected, required, or suggested levels of involvement for individuals, are these levels explicit, and do these levels change? What attempts are made by software designers to construct individuals' roles within the application (roles can refer to accountability, opportunities for role taking, and emergent roles), and how does this affect individuals' activities? How does the group-level activity appear to the individual? Who is included in the group and how are outsiders excluded, segregated, or otherwise distinguished? What are the time frames for retaining relevant accounts, is there an explicit "expiration date," and what kinds of access do group members (and others) have to these records?

***

Phillips, N. (1994). *Managing international teams.* Burr Ridge, IL: Irwin
    Professional Publishing, 219 pages.

According to Phillips, the changing business environment has created the need for international teams. In order to lead these teams effectively, managers must be capable of accessing and integrating information that comes to them through multiple cultural filters. They will need to understand different cultural perspectives and be able to adjust their decision-making and leadership style accordingly. The book aimed to describe the cultural issues raised by increasing globalization, to explain the effect of different national cultures on management styles, and to suggest ways of maximizing the potential of teams drawn from different nationalities. This book does not address issues specifically related to geographical dispersion, but it does provide information on the leadership styles of differing cultures. That information could be helpful to individuals leading geographically dispersed teams whose members come from diverse cultures.

***

Postmes, T., Spears, R., & Lea, M. (1998). Breaching or building social
    boundaries? *Communication Research, 25*(6), 689-709.

This article reviewed a series of studies that examine the effects of computer-mediated communication on social influences (such as norms, stereotypes, and boundaries) in teams. The authors concluded that certain configurations of technology may accentuate some of these social influences. The very aspects of computer-mediated communication, the authors argued, that are traditionally thought to free group members from social influences (for example, anonymity) may actually serve to reinforce a number of social boundaries, including attraction and commitment to the group, conformity to group norms, stereotyping, and ethnocentrism.

* * *

Raisinghani, M. S., Ramarapu, N. K., & Simkin, M. G. (1998). The impact of technology on cooperative work groups. *Information Systems Management, 15*(5), 40-47.

This article examined the uses of computers as an aid to collaborative work in teams, and is based on the assumption that it is possible to merge an understanding of technology with an understanding of group dynamics. The authors defined teams as being distinguishable by their names and memberships, their interaction behavior, their influence on others, their social context, and their identity within the larger organizational or economic environment. One context that can define teams is their use of computer-supported cooperative work (CSCW), which is the "use of computers in cooperative, coordinated, and collaborative work teams under various conditions of task, time, and space." The CSCW context influences many group-dynamics characteristics. CSCW allows teams to cross barriers of time and space (logic and order are changed; people can "talk" at once, not at all, or in illogical order; and members can go back in time by accessing computer storage and memory). CSCW helps team members overcome social and psychological barriers because social cues are lacking (members do not receive status, nonverbal, or personality cues) that may have both positive and negative effects on communication. CSCW also overcomes social inhibitions, encourages communication across social or psychological boundaries, and deregulates social behavior. People tend to be less concerned with being liked and more focused on the task. CSCW systems have created contexts that did not exist previously, the authors argued, and also affect group performance. It was hypothesized that CSCW improved task performance, overcame time and space constraints, increased information access, and facilitated conflict resolution.

* * *

Reinig, B. A., Briggs, R. O., Shepherd, M. M., Yen, J., & Nunamaker, J. F., Jr. (1995). Affective reward and the adoption of group support systems: Productivity is not always enough. *Journal of Management Information Systems, 12,* 171-185.

The purpose of this study was to develop and validate an instrument measuring affective reward concerning use of group support systems (GSS). Although recent research suggests that GSS can increase group effectiveness, another common finding is that users of GSS feel less personal and emotional

satisfaction with the process of completing a task using GSS. This disaffec-
tion may lead to resistance of GSS technology or limit its long-term effectiveness. The authors measured affective reward based on interviews with GSS
facilitators and observations of participants. It was hypothesized that participants in a more highly competitive task and participants who have difficult
preset goals would report a higher degree of affective reward. Neither of these
hypotheses was supported, but analyses showed that teams that attained their
goal reported higher affective reward. The report's 16-item instrument,
designed to evaluate changes in affective rewards among 275 undergraduates,
was presented in an appendix.

***

Scrivener, S. A. R. (Ed.). (1994). *Computer-supported cooperative work: The
multimedia and networking paradigm.* Brookfield, VT: Ashgate Publishing
Company, 304 pages.

This edited book has four sections, the first of which gave an introduction to computer-supported cooperative work (CSCW). Although there is no
agreed-upon definition of CSCW, it serves as a generic term that combines
the understanding of the way people work together in teams with the enabling
technologies of computer networking and associated hardware, software,
services, and techniques. CSCW includes all the ways that computers and
teams interact (including same time–same place, same time–different place,
different time–same place, and different time–different place). [That definition is broader than but also encompasses the GDT information reported in
this annotated bibliography.] The book's second and third sections dealt with
design considerations and specific case examples of teams that used desktop
teleconferencing. The final section considered, in general terms, CSCW
requirements and concepts, such as what further research was needed, environment requirements, the development of trust, and ways to implement
CSCW in organizations.

***

Shepherd, M. M., Briggs, R. O., Reinig, B. A., Yen, J., & Nunamaker, J. F.,
Jr. (1995). Invoking social comparison to improve electronic brainstorming. *Journal of Management Information Systems, 12,* 155-170.

Despite the fact that electronic brainstorming (EBS) teams, working
anonymously, tend to outperform manual brainstorming teams and nominal
teams, the anonymity provided in these teams may encourage *social loafing*—individuals expend less effort when their contributions are not specified.
This study presented two experiments conducted to examine the potential of

social comparison for reducing social loafing in EBS teams. In the initial study, conducted with 180 undergraduates randomly assigned to teams of five, the authors hypothesized than participants in an idea-generation task who received graphical reference information about the group average and their own levels of contribution would contribute more ideas than those participants who received no basis for social comparison. In the second study, conducted with 285 undergraduates also randomly assigned to teams of five, it was hypothesized that participants who received the same graphical reference information and were given a jocular and engaging task facilitator would produce a greater number of original ideas than participants with the same graphical feedback but a neutral facilitator. The respective hypotheses were supported. Despite the fact that facilitator manipulation was small, the two forms for enhancing social comparison (graphical references and facilitation) led to a 63 percent increase in generated ideas.

$$* * *$$

Short, J., Williams, E., & Christie, B. (1976). *The social psychology of telecommunications*. New York: John Wiley, 205 pages.

Two-way telecommunication has been with us for more than a hundred years; in 1976, when this book was written, newly available telecommunication devices already included group audio systems, video-telephones, conference television systems, and computer-mediated conferencing systems. This book documented the authors' telecommunications-impact model and described research they conducted using that model.

The model has four stages: amount, type allocation, mode allocation, and location change. The amount stage deals with the amount of communication within the organization. The type allocation stage deals with how that communication occurs using different telecommunications media and the adequacy and effectiveness of the various media used for communication. The mode-allocation stage attempts to predict which type of communication will be selected given geographical separation. The location-change stage attempts to predict the nature and extent of locational change due to the increased onset of telecommunications. Using a variety of surveys, the authors concluded that the outcome of meetings can be significantly affected by the medium of communication used. They found that in many situations, such as problem-solving interactions, the omission of visual nonverbal cues had little effect on the outcome. However, they did find that previous personal relationships were a mediating factor. The authors suggested that when there needs to be an inspection of fixed objects or interaction involving conflicts, negotiations, and disciplinary actions, the best communications medium is face-to-face. Forming impressions of others and giving information can be accomplished using video. Problem solving, information seeking, policy making, discussion of ideas, and delegation can be allocated to audio.

* * *

Snow, C. C., Davison, S. C., Snell, S. A., & Hambrick, D. C. (1996, Spring). Use transnational teams to globalize your company. *Organizational Dynamics*, pp. 50-67.

   This two-year, worldwide study of successful transnational teams examined how such teams are designed and managed to help their firms pursue global business strategies. The study was conducted in three phases. In the first phase, researchers identified successful transnational teams and interviewed more than a hundred team members and their leaders in thirteen companies. The second phase of the study was a questionnaire survey. Researchers designed two questionnaires, one for the team leader and the other for team members, and submitted them to thirty-five transnational teams. The questionnaire data were used to develop profiles of each team in the areas of mission, stage of development, staffing, leadership, decision-making, training, and performance. The study's third phase was a demonstration project in which human resource specialists from a specific company worked closely with two members of the research team to develop a practical, four-stage approach for improving team effectiveness. That approach was put to use in the company's transnational research and development and marketing teams. Beyond its research into transnational team effectiveness, the article also elaborated on team cultures at the national, corporate, and occupational levels, and discussed how effective transnational teams directly confront multicultural issues and search for ways to resolve them.

* * *

Solomon, C. M. (1998, November). Building teams across borders. *Global Workforce*, *3*(6), 13-17.

   Within the larger context of global, intercultural teams, this article discussed the importance of understanding rules, communicating, and cultivating leadership and cultural and functional diversity in geographically dispersed, technology-assisted teams. The author suggested that the advantages of global teams include less redundancy across teams, 24-hour productivity, and an increased depth of knowledge through cross-cultural and cross-functional diversity. The author made several recommendations: the team champion should have authority to select the appropriate team members; the team should have measurable goals that are discussed and established at the early stages of team existence; meetings should have structured objectives and agendas; appropriate lines of communication need to be discussed; and cultural differences and language difficulties must be understood. In addition, team members must realize that effective communication requires a certain amount of experience. Finally, the author argued that members must share or rotate leadership roles and be cognizant of roles outside the team that compete for member time.

***

Storck, J., & Sproull, L. (1995). Through a glass darkly: What people learn in videoconferences. *Human Communication Research, 22,* 197-219.

These researchers investigated what students in traditional classroom settings and in video-mediated settings learned about their colleagues, how they formed impressions of each other, and what information they used in forming those impressions. Based on previous research and theoretical arguments concerning the effects of various physical characteristics of videoconferences on the salience of important personal information, the authors hypothesized that people working in a face-to-face setting learn more about their colleagues, judge the quality of colleagues' work more accurately, form more positive impressions of their colleagues, and use more kinds of information in forming impressions of their colleagues than those who work together via videoconference. In an engineering classroom (with three on-site students) outfitted with videoconference monitors and audio equipment for two teams of remote students (one team of fourteen and one team of eight), the authors measured class performance and the impressions class colleagues formed of each other. They found that although remote students performed equally well in the class, students formed more positive impressions of their face-to-face colleagues than their video-mediated colleagues. In addition, those students who interacted only via video used fewer kinds of information to form impressions, and they appeared to rely on communication competence rather than task competence to form impressions. In conclusion, the authors offer some preliminary guidelines for the use of video technology, including videoconference etiquette, considering the suitability of the video medium for different types of tasks, and planning opportunities for face-to-face meetings to complement videoconferences.

***

Straus, S. G. (1996). Getting a clue: The effects of communication media and information distribution on participation and performance in computer-mediated and face-to-face groups. *Small Group Research, 27,* 115-142.

This study tested the assumption that computer-mediated communication (CMC) overcomes some of the process losses in teams because it fosters equal participation in discussions. Specifically, hypotheses addressed whether extraversion, the degree to which a person is outgoing and assertive rather than shy and inhibited, is related to the amount of participation; whether GDT members using CMC participated more equally than those meeting face-to-face; whether GDTs share more uniquely held information; and whether this sharing leads GDTs to outperform CLTs. It was also hypothesized that GDT members would be less satisfied with the process overall. One hundred sixty-two undergraduate students (74% male) participated in fifty-four three-person teams. The participants' extraversion was assessed using an eight-item survey that asked them the extent to which adjectives like "outspoken" and "assertive" described them. Twenty-eight teams communicated using computer conferencing and twenty-six teams met face-to-face. Unique task-relevant information was distributed equally across group members in twenty-seven teams and to a single member in twenty-seven teams. Results suggested that extraversion was related to the amount of participation in GDTs; those members ranked higher on extraversion participated more. Compared to CLTs, GDTs had more equal participation among members, but there were still more dominant and less dominant speakers. GDTs were not more likely to share uniquely held information than were CLTs, and GDTs did not outperform CLTs. GDT members were less satisfied with the process. Additionally, it took GDTs longer to complete the task, and they used fewer words in communicating the solution.

* * *

Straus, S. (1997). Technology, group process, and group outcomes: Testing the connections in computer-mediated and face-to-face groups. *Human-Computer Interaction, 12,* 227-266.

Based on data collected in an earlier study comparing the processes and outcomes of 243 undergraduate students divided into thirty-six computer-mediated teams of various size and thirty-six face-to-face three-person teams, this study investigated the effect of communication media on group processes and the subsequent effects of group processes on group cohesiveness, satisfaction, and productivity. It was hypothesized that computer-mediated GDTs would show greater task focus, less nonessential communication, and less supportive communication than would CLTs. But contrary to research suggesting that GDTs are less inhibited and "flame" more (to *flame* means to attack by e-mail), the author argued that hostile communication is actually rare and a minimum of personal attacks is expected in both types of teams. Despite research claiming that GDTs work with more equal participation, the author claimed that equalized participation could be a result of computer mediation limiting communication of all members. GDTs were also expected to exhibit lower cohesiveness because of higher task focus, less nonessential communication, less supportive communication and more disagreement, and have lower satisfaction because of excessive task focus.

The respective teams performed three separate tasks: idea generation, critical thinking, and judgment (the level of interdependence required for the tasks ranged from low to high). Team interactions were coded on the process variables, while cohesiveness and satisfaction were measured by self-report. Productivity was measured according to the number of original ideas in the idea-generation task, the number of questions answered in the intellective task, and the number of issues resolved in the judgment task. GDTs had higher task focus, more disagreement, more equalized participation, and more supportive communication than did CLTs. The greater nonessential communication and disagreement in GDTs explained the negative impact on cohesiveness. Communication media did not affect productivity through any of the group processes, a finding that did little to clarify the productivity differences previously reported between GDTs and CLTs. However, the results did cast doubt on the arguments that computer mediation increases depersonalization (leading to personal attacks) and that equalized participation increases productivity, satisfaction, or cohesiveness.

* * *

Sundstrom, E. (Ed.). (1999). *Supporting work team effectiveness: Best management practices for fostering high performance.* San Francisco: Jossey-Bass, 400 pages.

This edited book described how managers can create an environment and provide support for the team from outside the team. The authors divided teams into six kinds: production, service, management, project, action or performing, and parallel. Such topics as team structure, leaders' roles, and facilities, as well as systems for staffing communication, measurement, information, training, and rewards, were covered. Although all chapters contained helpful information for managers involved with GDTs, one particular chapter on communication technologies applies directly to GDTs. In this chapter, the authors discussed how electronic collaboration technologies provide communication channels, structure deliberation, and afford access to external information, allowing GDTs to share information, generate ideas, and make and document decisions.

* * *

Townsend, A. M., DeMarie, S. M., & Hendrickson, A. R. (1996). Are you ready for virtual teams? *Human Resources Management, 41*(9), 123-126.

This article identified five factors that make the GDT a powerful way of working: (1) GDTs allow organizations to build effective teams from personnel that might not otherwise be available to work together; (2) GDTs enhance the availability of resources from outside the organization, for example, by using an external consultant on the team; (3) GDTs allow organizations to hire and retain the best people regardless of where they are located; (4) team membership can adapt to fit needs; and (5) GDTs can be empowered through software products designed to enhance collaboration. Before the power of GDTs can be tapped, however, teams need training in the use of technology, communicating over a distributed medium, and collaboration.

* * *

Townsend, A. M., DeMarie, S. M., & Hendrickson, A. R. (1998). Virtual teams: Technology and the workplace of the future. *Academy of Management Executive, 12*(3), 17-29.

This article reviewed what is known about GDTs. Such teams are becoming more important due to five organizational factors: (1) flat or horizontal organizational structures, (2) interorganizational cooperation and competition, (3) expectations regarding worker participation, (4) shift from production to service/knowledge work environments, and (5) globalization. GDTs depend on technology for meetings and for accomplishing their business. These technologies include desktop videoconferencing systems, collaborative software systems, the Internet, and company intranets. Because of their structure, use of technology, and functional roles (which lead to changes in work and interaction), GDTs have different team-building needs from CLTs. For example, GDTs' members need ways to express themselves and understand others in a dispersed environment, they need team-participation skills, they need to be proficient in advanced technology, and they need to be accustomed to dealing with group members who are very different from each other. Finally, the authors gave some tips for capitalizing on GDTs, including consciously (as opposed to serendipitously) building teams (both within the group itself and structurally changing the organization); putting in place mechanisms and expectations for direction and control; carefully defining the team's role and function; carefully developing the team's technical systems (its infrastructure); developing teams and team members to work in a dispersed environment; helping members deal with challenges and obstacles; and dealing with such team-related issues as trust, cohesion, stress, and burnout.

***

Viega, J. F., & Dechant, K. (1997). Wired world woes (www.help). *Academy of Management Executive, 11*(3), 73-79.

This report, drawn from the annual survey of members of this journal's advisory board, revealed a good deal of information technology-related angst. Three hundred fifty executives were surveyed (average age 44, with 33% of the respondents female). It was found that executives used the following information technology (IT): e-mail (90.1%), voice mail (88.3%), fax (81.5%), Internet (52.8%), cellular phone (45.7%), and pager (12.7%). Additionally, executives reported that IT has not made their lives better, just busier (58%); IT's ability to add value is vastly overrated (55.3%); IT is seemingly out of date the moment it is taken out of the box (54.6%); IT wastes as much time as it saves (54.3%); IT-enabled communication produces more misunderstandings than does real-time human conversation (54%); IT has caused work relationships to deteriorate (50.8%); IT means serious information redundancy and overload (50%); IT creates a 24-hour office, leaving little time for self, friends, and family (45.9%); IT has caused the work environment to become too cold and impersonal (43.8%); and IT is by far the most abused managerial tool (42.1%).

***

Walther, J. (1994). Anticipated ongoing interaction versus channel effect on relational communication in computer-mediated interaction. *Human Communication Research, 20,* 473-493.

In this study, Walther tested the paradoxical finding that members of long-term GDTs express more personal statements in their initial electronic meeting than do members of GDTs that will be together only for a short time. He hypothesized that anticipation of future interactions drives this finding and that such anticipation is stronger in long-term GDTs than it is in CLTs. He further hypothesized that this anticipated future interaction predicts immediacy and affection, similarity and depth, receptivity and trust, composure and relaxation, and social orientation. To test his ideas, Walther recruited 114 students to participate in three-person teams. Some were told that they would only meet with this particular team once, while others were told that they would meet with their team continuously over six weeks. Some groups met face-to-face, while others met using synchronous or asynchronous computer-mediated communication. The author found that GDT members' anticipation of future interaction was more influenced by longevity than was the anticipation among CLT members. Furthermore, the author found that anticipated future interaction does predict such things as immediacy and affection, similarity and depth, receptivity and trust, and composure and relaxation (but not social orientation) when comparing asynchronous GDTs with CLTs. When comparing synchronous GDTs with CLTs, the hypotheses were only partly supported, which suggested that the impersonal effects found in early one-shot experiments may be due to the unrealistic nature of the experiments rather than to the effects of the technology.

∗∗∗

Walther, J. B. (1995). Relational aspects of computer-mediated communication: Experimental observations over time. *Organization Science, 6,* 186-203.

The author argued that time plays a crucial role in computer-mediated communication among teams. As CLTs and GDTs develop over time, the frequency at which members of the two types of teams transmit relational information to one another is similar. This social information-processing hypothesis opposes media-richness and social-presence theories, which state that computer-mediated communication is less able to pass along information about interpersonal relationships. To test this alternative hypothesis, ninety-six undergraduate students were randomly assigned to one of sixteen computer-mediated teams or to one of sixteen face-to-face teams, then compared at three different times during an extended decision-making task on several relational communication dimensions (for example, immediacy/affection, similarity/depth, composure, formality, and dominance). Because all of the study's seven hypotheses were either only partially supported or fully rejected, this study raised more questions about relational communication than it answered. However, two suggestions that move against conventional thought on asynchronous computer-mediated teamwork were offered: (1) teams with extended histories may be able to pass relational information across narrower and narrower bandwidths, and (2) teams that can communicate and coordinate implicitly through computer mediation may be able to bypass the team management procedures that hinder CLTs.

∗∗∗

Walther, J., & Anderson, J. (1994). Interpersonal effects in computer-mediated interaction. *Communication Research, 21,* 460-488.

In this study, researchers used meta-analytic procedures to test their hypotheses regarding the moderating effect of time limits on socio-emotional communication during computer-mediated communication. Specifically, they hypothesized that time limits are related to a lower proportion of socially oriented communication and to a greater proportion of antagonistic and negative communication, in comparison to no time limits. Based on a meta-analysis of twenty-one studies investigating socio-emotional tone, the authors found evidence to support the notion that groups operating under time constraints do show a lesser proportion of socially oriented communication than groups free of time constraints. The results of meta-analytic tests on fourteen studies examining negative communication did not support the hypothesized relationship between time limits and antagonistic and negative communication.

* * *

Wardell, C. (1998, November). The art of managing virtual teams: Eight key lessons. *Harvard Management Update*, pp. 4-5.

Based on discussions with business executives and team experts, these lessons are directed toward managers leading GDTs. The first of these lessons is to make sure that GDT managers have a handle on effective basic team strategies before approaching GDT strategies. GDTs need a clear mission and must test assumptions about everything, from scheduling to the meanings of words. Managers must encourage heavy communication to keep team members from feeling isolated and to establish trusting relationships. GDT leaders should consider finding allies in important positions and learn how different members of project teams may want to be compensated. Efforts to watch for conflict are necessary, as are creative strategies for managing conflict. GDTs must also develop ways to learn from experience to enhance future effectiveness.

* * *

Warkentin, M. E., Sayeed, L., & Hightower, R. (1997). Virtual teams versus face-to-face teams: An exploratory study of a web-based conference system. *Decision Sciences, 28,* 975-996.

The objective of this research was to compare relationship building between teams meeting in a face-to-face environment with teams meeting in an asynchronous environment. Seventy-two individuals were divided into thirteen GDTs and eleven CLTs. Individuals in the asynchronous meeting environment were novices. Researchers found that participants meeting face-to-face had stronger relational links than those using the asynchronous meetings. Members who met face-to-face rated their teams higher in terms of cohesion, perceptions of the group interaction process, and satisfaction with outcomes. However, teams in both conditions exchanged information equally effectively, and the expected link between relational links and information exchange did not appear.

***

Weisband, S. P., Schneider, S. K., & Connolly, T. (1995). Computer-mediated communication and social information: Status salience and status differences. *Academy of Management Journal, 38,* 1124-1151.

The object of the three studies reported in this paper was to determine whether GDTs are less prone to domination by high-status individuals than are CLTs. In all three studies, researchers used graduate and undergraduate business students to test hypotheses. The first study used thirty-four three-person teams (two MBA students and one BA student). Group members met each other before the task and knew who was a graduate and who was an undergraduate. In the second study, group composition was manipulated. Of the thirty-five teams, some were made up of two MBA students and one undergraduate. Others were made up of two undergraduates and one graduate student. Additionally, although they were introduced to one another, the GDT members were not identified in regard to class rank. In the third study, there was one face-to-face condition similar to the first study. There were also three distributed conditions: teams made up of two graduate students and one undergraduate who were identified, teams made up of two graduate students and one undergraduate who were anonymous, and teams made up of three members exhibiting empathic abilities. In all three studies, high-status members (MBA students) participated more in group discussions than did low-status members (undergraduate students). This finding held in GDTs, when high-status members were in the majority or in the minority, and when group members were anonymous.

***

Wilson, J. M., George, J., Wellings, R. S., with Byham, W. C. (Eds.). (1994). Virtual teams in virtual organizations: A look at the future. *Leadership trapeze: Strategies for leadership in team-based organizations* (pp. 249-264). San Francisco: Jossey-Bass, 286 pages.

This chapter describes the challenge of leading GDTs, which are more fluid and flexible than traditional CLTs. The authors include such challenges as: the leader has little or no "position power"; conflicts arise over team member time and resource requirements; organizational boundaries are unclear; time and organizational pressures abound; team members don't know one another; and team members often are independent and self-motivated. The remainder of the chapter presented strategies, tasks, and responsibilities to help leaders start, maintain, and disband a GDT. In closing, the authors stated that GDT leaders do not need new skills but rather a more advanced application of team-leadership skills already being used with CLTs.

***

World Wide Web Citations

Traditionally, annotated bibliographies have only included printed materials. Print materials such as books and periodicals are typically subjected to at least a rudimentary peer review process. That gives researchers and writers some measure of quality assurance. Print sources are also inherently stable and, in most cases, readily available in local public and university libraries. Annotated bibliographies review literature that, presumably, is accessible to readers who want to pursue the source materials.

However, the explosive growth of the Internet and, in particular, the increasing popularity of the World Wide Web indicates that many people are adopting on-line searches and sources as a primary means of retrieving information. Some reasons behind this movement include the relative ease, speed, and convenience of on-line searches as compared to library searches.

Convenience and speed are powerful enticements, but the Internet poses special problems to researchers. Chief among these problems is the lack of peer review for Internet postings (which anyone can make regardless of quality or standing). Another problem is the unstable nature of Web sites, which can literally appear or disappear overnight without history or trace. During the last year we have found several articles or position papers posted on the Web only to have them disappear later.

Despite these problems, we thought it would be a mistake not to acknowledge and even cite some of the information we have found on-line while compiling this bibliography. Some of these sites were hosted by consultants, others by colleges and universities. The citations we have chosen were available on the Web at the time this book went to press. We must also note that this short list is not inclusive. We encourage our readers to seek on-line information regarding geographically dispersed teams using the tools at their disposal. At the same time, we strongly recommend that readers determine who posted the material and what their expertise and profession is when judging the validity of the material, and that traditional printed materials be used to supplement knowledge gained through on-line searches.

Andres, H. P. (1996). *The impact of communication medium on software development performance: A comparison of face-to-face and virtual teams.* School of Business Administration, Portland State University. http://hsb.baylor.edu/ramsower/ais.ac.96/papers/virtteam.htm

This site carried an article written by Andres that described a research experiment designed to explore the effect and richness of communication mediums (richness refers to the extent to which a communication medium can provide immediate feedback, the number of cues and channels utilized, back-channeling cues, and socio-emotional content in a communication session) on the completion of a task (in this case, a software development project). Andres hypothesized that the face-to-face environment will experience a greater degree of software project success in task outcomes than will the videoconferencing environment, and the videoconferencing environment will experience a greater degree of software project success in psychosocial outcomes than experienced in the face-to-face environment.

∗∗∗

Gould, D. (n.d.). *Virtual organization.* http://www.seanet.com/%7edaveg/#leadership

This Web page, maintained by David Gould, was based upon his dissertation completed at Seattle University, Seattle, WA. This information on the site focused on various aspects of virtual organizations, such as organizational structure, leadership, collaboration, teams, technology, methods, and learning. The site provided results of his dissertation, "Leadership in Virtual Teams," and discussed factors influencing virtual teams.

∗∗∗

Kimball, L. (n.d.). *Boundaryless facilitation: Leveraging the strengths of face-to-face groupware tools to minimize group process.* http://www.tmn.com/~lisa/bnd2.htm

Kimball is part of the Metasystems Design Group, Inc., and Catalyst Consulting Team. On this Web site she shared Metasystems' experience with how the virtual environment creates challenges for working with teams and for the teams themselves. After describing an expanded paradigm of facilitation for virtual teams, the author provided a number of suggestions for relationship building in the virtual environment. Kimball also discussed the purpose of divergent conversations (to generate the most creative, highest quality, and most exhaustive set of ideas for a particular question, issue, or effort) and convergent conversations (to organize and prioritize a group's thinking, for example). The article closed by discussing how to sustain effective action.

***

Kimball, L. (n.d.). *Managing virtual teams.*
   http://www.tmn.com/~lisa/teams/matrix.htm

   This site contained four sections: Developing the team's communication strategy, Team effectiveness strategies, Choosing media for team communications, and Ten key elements to manage to make virtual teams more effective. Each section raised a number of questions virtual teams should address and offered recommendations.

***

Line, L. (1997). Virtual engineering teams: Strategies and implementation. *Electronic Journal of Information Technology in Construction.*
   http://www.itcon.org/1997/3/paper.htm

   This paper described a strategy for companies that want to organize GDTs. Because GDT members must balance technological and social issues, the author offered five basic elements that need to be addressed when creating a GDT strategy. First, at the start of the project, companies must establish a rationale for why a GDT is being implemented and make clear the strategic reasoning behind forming the GDT to the executive level, the group's managers, and the group's members. Second, a technical infrastructure tailored to the needs of the team must be in place to support the GDT. The team's needs include access to project information, access to common reference information, support for rich technical and human communication, support for human interaction, and support for coordination. The infrastructure must be ubiquitous, concurrent, stable, and conceptually simple and user-friendly—not piecemeal solutions or of haphazard design. Third, work structure must be designed and take into account both formal information exchange and informal communication needs and relations. Fourth, organizations need a system that ensures coaching and continuous learning for the group and its members, both in terms of the project itself and the technology the group is using. Finally, for full collaboration, group members need to be fully empowered through an open philosophy (all information is available to all employees) and a basic attitude of cooperation, as opposed to competitive individualism.

***

Reimus, B. (n.d.). *Knowledge sharing within management consulting firms. Report on how U.S.-based management consultancies deploy technology, use groupware and facilitate collaboration.*
http://www.kennedyinfo.com/mc/gware.html

This Web site included a 15-page article that discussed the way that management consultancies think about and apply technology within their own organizations. The author discussed the role of technology in providing a competitive advantage (especially in capturing best practices) and the types of technology use and return on investment for technology. After identifying some of the challenges faced by consultancies using technology (behavior, incentives to encourage sharing and security, and confidentiality), the author concluded by stating that consultancies (both expert- and methodology-driven) that use technology for information sharing will increasingly have an advantage over those that do not. While the article is not specifically about GDTs, the issues it raised and the information it provided is directly applicable.

***

Spargo, L., & Kelsey, B. (1997). *How two universities crossed the border.* School of Administration and Information Management, Ryerson Polytechnic University, Toronto, Ontario, Canada.
http://www.twnic.net/inet96/c8/c8_1.htm

The two objectives of this study were to determine how GDTs differ from CLTs and to see if Tuckman's (1965; see reference list) well-known model of group processes, developed using traditional teams, would apply to GDTs. To do this, researchers analyzed the team processes of eighteen collaborative project GDTs involving 108 telecommunications students at two universities. In comparison to CLTs, researchers found that (1) GDTs are far more stressful and time-consuming; (2) complexity of group dynamics over a distance was greater; (3) frustrations were harder to express; (4) there was a noticeable lack of social interaction; (5) there was no body language to add context and depth to what was being written; (6) the ability to write meaningful messages and the need to be effective communicators were seen as being critical success factors in working electronically; (7) feelings of disappointment, powerlessness, and hostility were reported as a result of unanswered e-mail or to research contributions; (8) delays caused by technical difficulties or conflicting priorities resulted in teams losing their focus; (9) there were difficulties in developing group consensus; (10) there was no casual talk that could be used to develop mutual understanding and so trust was hard to establish; and (11) it was hard to get a "feel" for the remote group members and what they really wanted.

Regarding the second objective, the research revealed that an existing model of face-to-face group development can be applied to GDTs. These teams do not appear to develop in the same fashion as predicted by the model, however, but in a unique temporal sequencing. The results show that, contrary to what Tuckman (1965) proposed (that small teams progress sequentially through development stages characterized by forming, storming, and norming), the GDTs experienced forming and norming behaviors well in advance of any storming behaviors. In fact, some norming events actually seemed to occur before the forming events did and certain storming activities were beginning even after the last performing activities had started. The authors concluded that while Tuckman's model was able to describe what went on in the teams, these GDTs experienced different developmental sequences from what the model describes.

***

Author Index

Title Index

CENTER FOR CREATIVE LEADERSHIP
New Releases, Best-sellers, Bibliographies, and Special Packages

NEW RELEASES

IDEAS INTO ACTION GUIDEBOOKS

Ongoing Feedback: How to Get It, How to Use It Kirkland & Manoogian (1998, Stock #400) .... $6.95 *

Reaching Your Development Goals McCauley & Martineau (1998, Stock #401) .... $6.95 *

Becoming a More Versatile Learner Dalton (1998, Stock #402) .... $6.95 *

Giving Feedback to Subordinates Buron & McDonald-Mann (1999, Stock #403) $6.95

Choosing Executives: A Research Report on the Peak Selection Simulation Deal, Sessa, & Taylor
(1999, Stock #183) $20.00

Coaching for Action: A Report on Long-term Advising in a Program Context Guthrie (1999,
Stock #181)... $20.00

The Complete Inklings: Columns on Leadership and Creativity Campbell (1999, Stock #343) $30.00

Geographically Dispersed Teams: An Annotated Bibliography (Sessa, Hansen, Prestridge, &
Kossler (1999, Stock #346) $20.00

High-Performance Work Organizations: Definitions, Practices, and an Annotated Bibliography
Kirkman, Lowe, & Young (1999, Stock #342) $20.00

Internalizing Strengths: An Overlooked Way of Overcoming Weaknesses in Managers Kaplan
(1999, Stock #182) $15.00

Positive Turbulence: Developing Climates for Creativity, Innovation, and Renewal
Gryskiewicz (1999, Stock #2031) $32.95

Selecting International Executives: A Suggested Framework and Annotated Bibliography
London & Sessa (1999, Stock #345) $20.00

Spirit and Leadership Moxley (1999, Stock #2035) $30.95

Workforce Reductions: An Annotated Bibliography Hickok (1999, Stock #344) $20.00

BEST-SELLERS

The Adventures of Team Fantastic: A Practical Guide for Team Leaders and Members Hallam
(1996, Stock #172) $20.00

Breaking Free: A Prescription for Personal and Organizational Change Noer (1997, Stock #271) $25.00

Breaking the Glass Ceiling: Can Women Reach the Top of America's Largest Corporations?
(Updated Edition) Morrison, White, & Van Velsor (1992, Stock #236A) $13.00

The Center for Creative Leadership Handbook of Leadership Development McCauley, Moxley,
& Van Velsor (Eds.) (1998, Stock #201) .... $65.00 *

CEO Selection: A Street-smart Review Hollenbeck (1994, Stock #164).............................. $25.00 *

Choosing 360: A Guide to Evaluating Multi-rater Feedback Instruments for Management
Development Van Velsor, Leslie, & Fleenor (1997, Stock #334) .... $15.00 *

A Cross-National Comparison of Effective Leadership and Teamwork: Toward a Global
Workforce Leslie & Van Velsor (1998, Stock #177) $15.00

Eighty-eight Assignments for Development in Place Lombardo & Eichinger (1989, Stock #136) .... $15.00 *

Enhancing 360-degree Feedback for Senior Executives: How to Maximize the Benefits and
Minimize the Risks Kaplan & Palus (1994, Stock #160) .... $15.00 *

Evolving Leaders: A Model for Promoting Leadership Development in Programs Palus & Drath
(1995, Stock #165) .... $15.00 *

Executive Selection: A Look at What We Know and What We Need to Know DeVries (1993,
Stock #321)... $20.00 *

Executive Selection: A Research Report on What Works and What Doesn't Sessa, Kaiser,
Taylor, & Campbell (1998, Stock #179) .... $30.00 *

Feedback to Managers (3rd Edition) Leslie & Fleenor (1998, Stock #178) .... $60.00 *

Four Essential Ways that Coaching Can Help Executives Witherspoon & White (1997, Stock #175) $10.00

A Glass Ceiling Survey: Benchmarking Barriers and Practices Morrison, Schreiber, & Price
(1995, Stock #161) $15.00

High Flyers: Developing the Next Generation of Leaders McCall (1997, Stock #293) $27.95

How to Design an Effective System for Developing Managers and Executives Dalton &
Hollenbeck (1996, Stock #158) .... $15.00 *

If I'm In Charge Here, Why Is Everybody Laughing? Campbell (1984, Stock #205) .... $9.95 *

If You Don't Know Where You're Going You'll Probably End Up Somewhere Else Campbell (1974, Stock #203) $9.95*

International Success: Selecting, Developing, and Supporting Expatriate Managers Wilson & Dalton (1998, Stock #180) $15.00*

Leadership Education: A Source Book of Courses and Programs Schwartz, Freeman, & Axtman (Eds.) (1998, Stock #339) $40.00*

Leadership Resources: A Guide to Training and Development Tools Schwartz, Freeman, & Axtman (Eds.) (1998, Stock #340) $40.00*

The Lessons of Experience: How Successful Executives Develop on the Job McCall, Lombardo, & Morrison (1988, Stock #211) $27.50

A Look at Derailment Today: North America and Europe Leslie & Van Velsor (1996, Stock #169) $20.00*

Making Common Sense: Leadership as Meaning-making in a Community of Practice Drath & Palus (1994, Stock #156) $15.00*

Making Diversity Happen: Controversies and Solutions Morrison, Ruderman, & Hughes-James (1993, Stock #320) $20.00

Managerial Promotion: The Dynamics for Men and Women Ruderman, Ohlott, & Kram (1996, Stock #170) $15.00

Managing Across Cultures: A Learning Framework Wilson, Hoppe, & Sayles (1996, Stock #173) $15.00

Maximizing the Value of 360-degree Feedback Tornow, London, & CCL Associates (1998, Stock #295) $42.95*

The New Leaders: Guidelines on Leadership Diversity in America Morrison (1992, Stock #238A) $18.50

Perspectives on Dialogue: Making Talk Developmental for Individuals and Organizations Dixon (1996, Stock #168) $20.00*

Preventing Derailment: What To Do Before It's Too Late Lombardo & Eichinger (1989, Stock #138) $25.00

The Realities of Management Promotion Ruderman & Ohlott (1994, Stock #157) $15.00*

Selected Research on Work Team Diversity Ruderman, Hughes-James, & Jackson (Eds.) (1996, Stock #326) $24.95

Should 360-degree Feedback Be Used Only for Developmental Purposes? Bracken, Dalton, Jako, McCauley, Pollman, with Preface by Hollenbeck (1997, Stock #335) $15.00*

Take the Road to Creativity and Get Off Your Dead End Campbell (1977, Stock #204) $9.95*

Twenty-two Ways to Develop Leadership in Staff Managers Eichinger & Lombardo (1990, Stock #144) $15.00

BIBLIOGRAPHIES

Formal Mentoring Programs in Organizations: An Annotated Bibliography Douglas (1997, Stock #332) $20.00

Management Development through Job Experiences: An Annotated Bibliography McCauley & Brutus (1998, Stock #337) $20.00

Selection at the Top: An Annotated Bibliography Sessa & Campbell (1997, Stock #333) $20.00*

Succession Planning: An Annotated Bibliography Eastman (1995, Stock #324) $20.00*

Using 360-degree Feedback in Organizations: An Annotated Bibliography Fleenor & Prince (1997, Stock #338) $15.00*

SPECIAL PACKAGES

Executive Selection (Stock #710C; includes 157, 164, 179, 180, 321, 333) $85.00

Guidebook Package (Stock #721; includes 400, 401, 402) $14.95

HR Professional's Info Pack (Stock #717C; includes 136, 158, 169, 201, 324, 334, 340) $100.00

Leadership Education and Leadership Resources Package (Stock #722; includes 339, 340) $70.00

New Understanding of Leadership (Stock #718; includes 156, 165, 168) $40.00

Personal Growth, Taking Charge, and Enhancing Creativity (Stock #231; includes 203, 204, 205) ... $20.00

The 360 Collection (Stock #720C; includes 160, 178, 295, 334, 335, 338) $75.00

Discounts are available. Please write for a Resources catalog. Address your request to: Publication, Center for Creative Leadership, P.O. Box 26300, Greensboro, NC 27438-6300, 336-286-4480, or fax to 336-282-3284. Purchase your publications from our on-line bookstore at **www.ccl.org/publications**. All prices subject to change.

*Indicates publication is also part of a package.

ORDER FORM

Or e-mail your order via the Center's on-line bookstore at www.ccl.org

Name _____ Title _____

Organization _____

Mailing Address _____
(street address required for mailing)

City/State/Zip _____

Telephone _____ _____ FAX _____
(telephone number required for UPS mailing)

Quantity	Stock No.	Title	Unit Cost	Amount

CCL's Federal ID Number
is 237-07-9591.

Subtotal

Shipping and Handling
(add 6% of subtotal with a $4.00 minimum;
add 40% on all international shipping)

NC residents add 6% sales tax; CA residents add
7.75% sales tax; CO residents add 6.1% sales tax

TOTAL

METHOD OF PAYMENT
(ALL orders for less than $100 must be PREPAID.)

❏ Check or money order enclosed (payable to Center for Creative Leadership).

❏ Purchase Order No. _____ (Must be accompanied by this form.)

❏ Charge my order, plus shipping, to my credit card:
  ❏ American Express ❏ Discover ❏ MasterCard ❏ VISA

ACCOUNT NUMBER: _____ EXPIRATION DATE: MO.____ YR.____

NAME OF ISSUING BANK: _____

SIGNATURE _____

❏ Please put me on your mailing list.

Publication • Center for Creative Leadership • P.O. Box 26300
Greensboro, NC 27438-6300
336-286-4480 • FAX 336-282-3284

Client Priority Code: R

fold here

_____

_____

_____

CENTER FOR CREATIVE LEADERSHIP
PUBLICATION
P.O. Box 26300
Greensboro, NC 27438-6300